CICERO
PRO MILONE

Edited with Introduction and Notes by

F. H. Colson

Formerly Headmaster of Plymouth College and late
Fellow of St. John's College, Cambridge

with Asconius' commentary appended

Published by Bristol Classical Press
General Editor: John H. Betts
(by arrangement with Macmillan & Co. Ltd.)

Cover illustration: Cicero from a portrait bust, Vatican Museums, Rome.

Printed in England
ISBN 0-906515-50-5

First published by Macmillan & Co. Ltd, (1893)

New edition (1980) published by Bristol Classical Press
with Asconius' commentary appended.

Bristol Classical Press
Department of Classics
University of Bristol
Wills Memorial Building
Queens Road
BRISTOL BS8 1RJ

CONTENTS

INTRODUCTION[1].

1. *Events before the Murder of Clodius.*

The events of the years preceding the trial of
Milo are amongst the best known in Roman History.
I therefore give only a very brief summary.

In 63 B.C. Cicero was consul; he discovered and
suppressed the Catilinarian conspiracy, had several of
the chief conspirators executed with doubtful legality,
and placed the aristocratic or republican party on a
strong basis by drawing the Senate and Knights
together.

In 62 Pompey who had been absent in the East
returned. On the whole the same state of affairs as
in the preceding year.

In 61 Cicero incurred the deadly enmity of
Publius Claudius (commonly called Clodius) Pulcher.
Clodius was tried for sacrilegiously intruding himself

---

[1] Our chief authority for the story of Clodius' murder and
Milo's trial is the invaluable commentary on the speech by
Q. Asconius Pedianus (born about B.C. 2). This consists of
an argument, several notes on allusions in the speech, and an
account of the result of the trial. There is also some account
of the events in Dion Cassius XL. 48 &c., Appian Bellum Civile
II. 20 &c. Compare also Plutarch's 'Cicero' and 'Pompey.'
Cicero's letters give us very little help for this time.
For Asconius' commentary, see Appendix p. 137 below.

in women's clothes into the rites of the "Bona Dea," to which only women were admitted. The alibi which he endeavoured to establish was overthrown by Cicero who also bitterly opposed him in the Senate.

In 60 Pompey became estranged from the Senate. He formed with Caesar and Crassus the coalition called the first triumvirate.

In 59 Caesar was consul and the Triumvirs were supreme. Glad of an opportunity to humiliate their opponents they lent their aid to Clodius in his schemes of vengeance on Cicero. As the first step to this Clodius was adopted into a Plebeian family, and thus qualified for the Tribuneship. At the end of the year Caesar went to Gaul.

In 58 Clodius was Tribune. He brought in a bill aimed against Cicero, inflicting banishment on anyone who had executed a citizen without trial. Clodius' bands ruled the streets; Pompey left Cicero to his fate, and he went into banishment.

In 57 Pompey, finding himself in danger from Clodius, promoted the recall of Cicero. This was accomplished in spite of the fierce opposition of Clodius. One staunch supporter of Cicero was the Tribune T. Annius Papianus Milo, son of T. Papius Celsus, and adopted by his mother's father T. Annius Luscus[2]. Milo followed Clodius' example in organ-

---

[2] Hence two at any rate of the *tria patrimonia* mentioned in § 95.

izing bands of armed slaves, who met Clodius' violence by counter violence. In consequence of the action which he took, he and Cicero became close friends. He endeavoured twice during this year to prosecute Clodius.

In 56 Clodius prosecuted Milo, who was defended by Pompey. The two gang-leaders after this subsided for some time. Signs of disunion between the Triumvirs showed themselves, but a reconciliation was patched up at the conference of Lucca. Cicero himself gave in his adherence to them, and the opposition as a whole submitted. Clodius was reconciled to Pompey.

In 55 Pompey and Crassus consuls. The Triumvirs supreme.

In 54 Julia, Pompey's wife and Caesar's daughter, died. The first signs of a breach appeared. Crassus went on an expedition to the East.

In 53 defeat and death of Crassus; riots between Clodius and Milo renewed, Milo being a candidate for the consulship (against Scipio and Hypsaeus, nominees of Pompey) and Clodius for the Praetorship. Cicero defended Milo when attacked in the Senate, as insolvent (de aere alieno Milonis).

In 52 on Jan. 18th Clodius and Milo met on the Appian Road near Bovillae, about 12 miles from Rome. Clodius with a small body of armed followers was returning from Aricia. Milo accompanied by his wife and her establishment and a large body of his own slaves was on his way to Lanuvium. The two chieftains passed each other, but their followers began to quarrel. In the scuffle Clodius was wounded and was taken into a tavern at Bovillae. He was dragged out by Milo's orders and killed, and his body was left in the Appian Road.

2.   *Events after the Murder.*

At this point we must go somewhat into detail. The body of Clodius was brought back to Rome the same evening. Great popular indignation was excited, and on the next day the corpse was carried to the Forum and exposed to public view. Two tribunes, Munatius Plancus and Pompeius Rufus, held a meeting and made inflammatory speeches. The corpse of Clodius at the instigation of Sextus Clodius was carried into the Curia and burnt on a funeral pyre of benches, tables and documents. The flames spread, and the Senate House itself was burnt down.

However the more sober part of the citizens may have regarded the murder, the destruction of the Senate House excited a reaction against the Clodians. Under its cover Milo, who had returned to Rome, ventured abroad and proceeded with his canvass. The mob meanwhile were clamouring for his trial. Their first object was to have the comitia held, for till this was done the courts could not sit and Milo could not be tried. The Senate appointed Lepidus 'interrex.' His house was besieged for five days by the mob who hoped[3] to induce him to hold the elections. Failing in this they clamoured for Pompey himself to become consul or dictator.

This in fact was the direction in which everything was tending. After several 'interreges' had been appointed and yet no elections could be held, the Senate resolved that the interrex for the time being together with the Tribunes and Pompey, should make provision for the public safety, and that Pompey should levy troops throughout Italy. Pompey acted with great promptitude[4] and some sort of order was at once restored. Both parties prepared for legal action : demands and counter demands were made for the examination by torture of the slaves of Clodius and Milo. The latter made some attempts to conciliate Pompey, but was mercilessly snubbed. A few[5] days before the beginning of March Pompey was appointed sole consul, a title which gave him the powers of a dictator without the name. He immediately proceeded to consult the Senate. The first resolution proposed was that the riots of January the

---

[3] It was not constitutional for the interrex first appointed to hold the *comitia*. He appointed a successor after 5 days, who was allowed to do so.

[4] *Qui quum summa celeritate praesidium comparasset*, Asc. 10.

[5] In 52, February had 23 days and was followed by an intercalary month of 28.

18th and the following days were prejudicial to the state, and that Milo should be tried under the existing laws 'extra ordinem.' The second half of this was vetoed; the first was carried, and Pompey was left to take what action he thought good. He at once brought before the comitia a new law 'de vi,' in which he proposed a special commission to investigate several riotous actions. Amongst them were mentioned the fray on the Appian Road, the burning of the Senate House, and the attack upon the house of Lepidus. He also proposed a law against bribery, in which the penalty was made more severe. In both cases[6] the form of proceedings was shortened. Three days were allowed for the examination of witnesses, one for the speeches for the prosecution (2 hours), and the defence (3 hours), and also for the verdict. The president of the court was to be chosen by the vote of the people from amongst the ex-consuls. The Judices were to be taken as usual from the three classes, 360 being empanelled by Pompey, of whom 81 were chosen by lot on the fourth day of the trial, and finally reduced to 51 by challenges.

Under this new law Milo was prosecuted by two nephews of Clodius, both of whom were called Appius, sons of an elder brother C. Clodius. The trial was fixed for the 4th April. Meanwhile the

---

[6] So Asconius 15 *utraque lex iubebat &c.* But probably the alteration in procedure extended to other courts as well, Madv. Opusc. Ac. ii. 246.

feeling against Milo increased. Pompey openly declared that he suspected him of worse designs, shut himself up in his grounds, and surrounded himself with a guard.

The trial began. The first witness was a Clodian Causinius Schola. Marcellus cross-examined him, but was subjected to such disorderly interruptions that he had to ask for protection. The consequence was that Pompey for the next two days brought a guard and kept order. On the 4th day of the trial the judges were finally chosen. The prosecution spoke for the allotted two hours. Pompey and his soldiers were present again and maintained silence, till Cicero rose to reply for Milo. The Clodians at once raised a clamour: Cicero lost his head and his speech proved a failure. Milo was condemned by 38 votes to 13. He was subsequently tried and condemned in 3 different courts for 'ambitus,' 'sodalicia' or unlawful associations, and 'vis.' He immediately went into exile at Massilia, and his property was sold to pay his debts.

The rest of his story can be shortly told. When Caesar recalled the other exiles, he refused to do the same for Milo, who in the year 48 at the invitation of Caelius, headed a band of slaves and was killed under the walls of a fort in the south of Italy.

3. *The political significance of Milo's trial.*

Milo was little more than a ruffian and a desperado, but his trial has more importance than appears at first sight. It is the first scene of the last act of the drama which ended at Pharsalia.

At the beginning of 52 the triumvirate was at the height of its power. Perhaps we should say Pompey rather than the triumvirate. It has often been pointed out that till the end of this decade the triumvirate, to the average Roman, meant Pompey rather than Caesar. Pompey was the 'dominus,' his colleagues were the 'advocati.' At the time of the death of Clodius this was especially the case, for Crassus was dead, and Caesar was face to face with Vercingetorix. But though the republican opposition was cowed, there was still an opposition and its most prominent member was Milo. Hypsaeus and Scipio, the candidates for the consulship were Pompey's nominees, and when Milo opposed them he was opposing Pompey.

There had been before this much talk of making Pompey dictator. Whether it be true or not, that Pompey fomented disorder, in order to make a dictator necessary, it may be assumed that those who promoted disorder played Pompey's game. And therefore when Milo murdered Clodius on the Appian Road and let all the demons of anarchy loose, he not only destroyed his own hopes of the consulship and established those of the Pompeian candidates, but he practically placed the dictatorship in Pompey's hand.

Pompey, as we have seen, did become dictator under the title of sole consul. But it is noticeable that this most unconstitutional step served to place him at the head of the constitutional party. We get little help from Cicero's correspondence for this year, but it is clear that just at this time[7] there was a rapprochement between Pompey and the Senate. He refused to receive the dictatorship from the mob, but accepted it from the Senate on the proposition of such staunch conservatives as Bibulus and Cato, and acquiesced in the title which they substituted for the hated name of dictator. From this time forward Pompey ceases to be associated with a revolutionary policy, and is installed as the leader of the republican party.

Let us now observe Cicero's position. I have no prepossessions in favour of his career as a politician, but I cannot but feel that he comes well out of the affair. Pompey was, as we have seen, extremely powerful: he was on better terms with Cicero's natural associates, than he had ever been. Cicero had every political motive for sacrificing Milo to Pompey, at any rate after a decent resistance. The only motive to draw him the other way was gratitude and an affection, genuine if misplaced, for Milo.

[7] v. especially Mommsen, Vol. iv. ch. 8 and 9.

Yet he adhered to his friend with a firmness which well deserves the praise[8] of Asconius, and the physical timidity which he showed at the trial only enhances the moral courage he showed both before and after. For the 'pro Milone,' in the form in which Cicero published it, is a bold speech. Under a thin veil of conventional compliment can be traced a bitter attack upon the Triumvir, which he cannot have failed to appreciate, unless indeed he was even more stupid than modern historians have represented him. He who afterwards winced under Cicero's tongue in the camp in Greece, cannot but have felt the irony in the first 3 sections of the speech. Still more offensive is the suggestion in section 21, that Pompey's only motive in proposing the commission was to appease the Clodians with a mere show of severity, while he trusted to the jury to acquit Milo. In sections 61—66, where he sneers at Pompey's 'diligentia[9],' he no doubt hits a weak place very hard, and above all, the passage in section 69, in which he foreshadows the coming events of the civil

---

[8] *Tanta tamen constantia ac fides fuit Ciceronis, ut non populi a se alienatione, non Cn. Pompeii suspicionibus, non periculo futurum ut sibi dies ad populum diceretur, non armis quae palam in Milonem sumpta erant, deterreri potuit a defensione eius, cum posset omne periculum suum et offensionem inimicae sibi multitudinis declinare, redimere autem Cn. Pompeii animum, si paulum ex studio defensionis remisisset,* Asc. 22.

[9] We need hardly suppose however with an ingenious German that in the words *diligentiam nimiam nullam putabam* § 66 there lurks a *double entendre* : 'I thought excessive carefulness nonsense.'

war and trusts that Pompey will not have to regret his present error, savours more of a threat than a warning. But the breach that was made between the two was soon mended. In the next year, before Cicero departed to Cilicia, he was on excellent terms with Pompey, and we have it on his own authority that throughout this crisis Pompey[10] showed the utmost tact and forbearance. Indeed though there may be something to blame, there is much to praise in Pompey's behaviour in this crisis. He dealt out even justice to all the rioters. Sextus Clodius suffered the same fate as Milo and in fact the Clodians came off worse in the long series of trials[11] than their opponents. It may be true that his new regulations as to judicial procedure gave a heavy blow to the power of forensic eloquence[12], but on the other hand, the prohibition of testimonials to character (laudationes), put an end to a very mischievous institution. People are perhaps as little likely to agree about Pompey as about Cicero. It is possible no doubt to represent his action during this year as a selfish and clumsy policy. It may be said that he

[10] Ad Fam. III. 10, 10 *qua denique ille facilitate, qua humanitate tulit contentionem meam pro Milone, adversantem interdum actionibus suis? quo studio providit ne quae me illius temporis invidia attingeret, cum me consilio, cum auctoritate, cum armis denique texit suis?*

[11] *in multitudine et celebritate iudiciorum,* Ad Fam. VII. 2, 4.

[12] Dial. de Or. 38 *primus haec* (i.e. *numerum dierum et patronorum) tertio consulatu Cn. Pompeius astrinxit, imposuitque veluti frenos eloquentiae.*

revenged a personal spite against Milo, that he played off the Clodians against the Senate till he gained the adherence of the latter, and then sacrificed his former allies to the vengeance of his new ones, and that his alliance with the Senate was only a preparation for the breach with Caesar. But it is also possible to think that while he knew that nothing but his regency could cope with anarchy, he really wished to rule through the senatorial and constitutional party : that he welcomed an opportunity of an alliance with them, but insisted on their cooperation in putting down disorder in whatever cause it was used, and that the price which the optimates paid for their reconciliation with him was the surrender of Milo to the punishment which he had so richly deserved.

4. *Personages connected with the trial.*

The 'quaesitor' appointed to preside at the trial was L. Domitius Ahenobarbus (§ 22); who had been consul in B.C. 54. He had been an opponent of the triumvirs, but from this time became a supporter of Pompey. In the civil war he held Corfinium against Caesar, and on surrendering was dismissed by him uninjured. He was killed at Pharsalia.

The leading opponents of Milo were the following. I. T. Munatius Plancus Byrsa, brother of L.

Munatius Plancus, the friend of Caesar, was tribune in the year of the trial. He took an active part in rousing the people against Milo. He is said to have fostered Pompey's suspicions of Milo, and threatened Cicero with impeachment. At the close of the year when he laid down his office he was accused under the 'Lex Pompeia.' Cicero prosecuted. Pompey endeavoured to protect him and violated his own rule by sending a 'laudatio.' He was however condemned to Cicero's great delight. He afterwards joined Caesar. He is never mentioned by name in the speech, but is alluded to in §§ 12, 14.

II. Q. Pompeius Rufus also tribune took much the same line as Plancus, though apparently with less insistence, as he was suspected at one time of having made a reconciliation with Cicero and Milo[13]. According to Dion Cass. (XL. 45), he was thrown into prison by the Senate during his tribunate. At the end of the year he was prosecuted by Caelius and condemned.

III. C. Sallustius Crispus, the famous historian, was also tribune and acted with Rufus, though less prominently. He did not take any part in the riot which led to the burning of the Senate House.

IV. Q. Metellus Scipio, a rival candidate of Milo for the consulship was the first to attack him formally in the Senate for the murder. Pompey married his daughter and on the 1st of August made

[13] **Asc. 21.**

him his colleague in the consulship. He was accused of bribery and acquitted.

V. Causinius Schola—a friend of Clodius (§ 46) was present at the murder and was the first and chief witness against Milo, as he had been the chief witness for Clodius in the 'Bona Dea' trial.

VI. Sextus Clodius, a man of low birth and a protégé of Clodius was his chief lieutenant during his life and headed the riot which ended in the burning of the Senate House. He was prosecuted for it and condemned (§§ 33, 90).

VII. Appius Clodius Pulcher (and his brother also named Appius) sons of C. Clodius, elder brother of Publius, were the prosecutors. They produced their uncle's slaves, who had passed into their possession, to be examined by torture. The elder brother spoke at the trial. M. Antonius (the future triumvir, who shortly after left for Gaul) and P. Valerius Nepos also spoke.

By far the most prominent supporter of Milo next to Cicero himself was

VIII. M. Caelius Rufus. He had been one of the lovers of Clodius' infamous sister Clodia, and had been prosecuted at the instigation of her and her brother and defended by Cicero. In 52 he also was tribune. He gave Milo an early opportunity of addressing a public meeting during which they were attacked by the Clodians and had both to escape in the disguise of slaves. He opposed the 'leges

Pompeiae' on the ground that they were virtually a 'privilegium' against Milo, and that the trial was being unduly hurried, and his resistance was so obstinate, that Pompey threatened to have recourse to arms.   After the trial he successfully accused, as we have seen, Pompeius Rufus and defended Saufeius, who had actually murdered Clodius under Milo's orders.   In 48 he summoned Milo from Massilia to his help and raised some disturbances in the south of Italy, during which he lost his life.   [A most interesting account of Caelius is to be found in Tyrrell's introduction to Cicero's letters, Vol. III.]

IX.   M. Porcius Cato certainly supported Milo before the trial[14] and was certainly one of the 'judices.' Velleius Paterculus (whose grandfather was one of the judges) declares[15] that he voted openly for him.   Asconius on the other hand says that it was not known which way he voted[16].

X.   Q. Hortensius the famous orator also supported Milo[17].   (§ 37.)

XI.   M. Marcellus, a close friend of Cicero, and the subject of the speech 'pro Marcello' had defended Milo when prosecuted by Clodius in 56.   He supported Milo throughout and cross-examined witnesses at the trial[18].

---

[14] Asc. 11.   [15] Vell. Pat. II. 47.   [16] Asc. 32.
[17] Asc. 11.   [18] Asc. 11, 27.

5. *Cicero's case and his treatment of it.*

Following the arrangement given by Cicero in the 'Partitiones Oratoriae' we may divide the Milo into four parts.

§ 1—23. (1) Principium or prooemium.

§ 24—29. (2) Narratio (statement of facts).

§ 30—91. (3) Confirmatio (proof).

§ 92—105. (4) Peroratio.

I. The prooemium of the Milo is a very important part of the speech. In it Cicero deals with

A. A possible fear that the troops stationed by Pompey were intended to secure a verdict against Milo.

B. The idea, that as Milo admitted the homicide, there could be no doubt as to his punishment.

C. The 'praejudicium' passed on the case by the Senate in their resolution that the murder of Clodius was injurious to the state.

D. The arrangements made by Pompey for the trial which were regarded as arguing a belief in his guilt, or a wish for his punishment.

A is disposed of in the first chapter. The orator apologises for his nervousness, which he attributes to the strangeness of the spectacle, not to any idea that the troops mean intimidation. What he says is probably true enough. There is no sufficient reason to doubt that the only object of the troops was to maintain order[19].

B, C, D are classed together by Cicero and he deals with them at considerable length. In regard to *B* his arguments may, at first sight, seem superfluous. If it was proved that Clodius was the 'insidiator,' there could not of course be any doubt that Milo deserved an acquittal. The historical and literary arguments which Cicero adduces to prove this obvious point are partly intended as mere ornaments to the speech : but it must also be remembered that they pave the way for § 72 etc., in which the orator virtually argues that, Clodius being a bad citizen, it was a meritorious act to assassinate him.

C. The 'praejudicium' of the Senate was no doubt a serious difficulty. Asconius found in the 'Acta' of the Senate a resolution that 'P. Clodii caedem contra rempublicam esse' and such a verdict on their own supporter was a clear hint to the jury that Milo must be surrendered to vengeance. Cicero meets it by a statement that the mere fact of killing Clodius had been approved of by the Senate, but that they felt that all cases of violence are regrettable and require to be sifted, however salutary the result[20]. He gives some force to this view by declaring that he voted for the

---

[19] Though in Lucan i. 320 &c. Caesar is represented as taking the other view *auso medias perrumpere milite leges.*
[20] Cp. Velleius Paterculus ii. 47 *Clodius exemplo inutili, sed facto salutari reipublicae iugulatus est.*

resolution himself on these grounds.   The suggestion that the existence of the special ' quaestio' showed the severity with which the Senate regarded the murder, is easily met by the fact that the ' quaestio' was not voted by the Senate at all.

D.   The undoubted opposition of Pompey is the fatal difficulty which meets Cicero at every step[21]. The opposer baffled by Cicero's explanation of the Senate's resolution is supposed to fall back on the plea that at any rate Pompey's motion at the comitia had prejudged the case, apparently because in that motion the fray was expressly described as "the murderous assault in which Clodius was killed[22]." Cicero meets this by pointing out that the very fact of demanding an enquiry into an undisputed act of homicide implies that the question whether the homicide is justifiable has still to be decided.   At the same time he evidently allows that Pompey's proposal of a special ' quaestio' would naturally be taken as a *prima facie* sign of his disfavour.   This he meets by the extraordinary suggestion that the new ' quaestio' was

---

[21] Vell. Pat. **II.** 47 *Milonem reum non magis invidia facti, quam Pompeii damnavit voluntas.*

[22] § 15 *tulit enim de caede, quae in Appia via facta esset, in qua P. Clodius occisus esset.*   But according to Asconius on § 14 the resolution in the Senate was even more definite. *Acta etiam totius illius temporis persecutus sum; in quibus cognovi pridie Kal. Mart. s.c. esse factum, P. Clodi caedem et incendium curiae et oppugnationem aedium M. Lepidi contra rempublicam factam; ultra relatum in Actis nihil.*   Still I can see no other meaning for the words.   Unless Pompey's *rogatio* reflected on Milo in some way in which the *Senatus-consultum* did not, the same argument would have served to meet both.

simply a subterfuge of Pompey's. He wished to appear faithful to his supposed friendship with Clodius, but was at the same time sure that the jury would do their duty and not condemn Milo. He goes on to show, what is probably true enough, that the selection of judges and president showed no prejudice[23]. On the whole however it is clear that Pompey's hostile attitude and his suspicions of Milo's designs were, throughout Cicero's difficulty, and it is a curious weakness in the speech[24], that in the midst of his plausible attempts to show that the Triumvir is neutral, he often lets slip some chance phrase which shows how the land really lay.

II. The 'narratio' is terse, clear and plausible[25]. In fact it may be said to have every merit except truthfulness. But such parts of it as are important to the case may be taken with the next section.

III. The 'confirmatio.' The main part of Milo's case, the 'causa' proper, takes the form of a dilemma; 'constat in re insidias esse: quaeritur uter utri insidias fecerit.' This dilemma is not merely logically unsound, but is absolutely untrue[26]—the fact being

---

[23] *Album quoque iudicūm qui de ea re iudicarent, Pompeius tale proposuit, ut nunquam neque clariores viros neque sanctiores propositos esse constaret,* Asc. 23.

[24] Cp. *quamvis atrociter ipse tulisset* § 21, *eius sedetis ultores* § 79, *a quibus tueri* (if right) § 102, and the whole tone of §§ 67—71.

[25] Ad Herenn. i. 14 *tres res convenit habere narrationem, ut brevis, ut dilucida, ut verisimilis sit.*

[26] 'If we may judge from the Cluentius and the Milo we should be inclined to say that whenever Cicero put his points with great apparent clearness in the form of a logical dilemma, he is likely to be cloaking a weak argument.' Tyrrell (iii. p. xlvii).

as we have seen that the meeting was accidental. We may divide the arguments on this part of the case as follows.

α. That Clodius was an 'insidiator.'

(1) Clodius had a motive for wishing to murder Milo, who would have been a formidable obstacle to him in his praetorship.

(2) Clodius had a personal hatred for Milo.

(3) Clodius regularly had recourse to violence; indeed he had actually declared his intention of murdering Milo.

(4) No satisfactory account is given of Clodius' movements before the murder.

(5) The place where the conflict took place was suitable to Clodius.

(6) Clodius' retinue was equipped for battle.

β. That Milo was not.

(1) Clodius' death was not to Milo's interest. His public career would have lost its prestige, if he had no one whose outrages he could repress.

(2) Milo had no personal hatred for Clodius.

(3) Milo never had recourse to violence against Clodius, though he had several excellent opportunities of killing him.

(4) A satisfactory account can be given of Milo's movements.

(5) Unsuitable to Milo.

(6) Milo's was not.

(7) Milo had a good reason for manumitting the slaves who were demanded for examination by torture, while the evidence which Clodius' slaves gave against Milo was worthless.

(8) Milo's conduct after the event was not that of a guilty man.

a is certainly not proved. Most of the arguments are of the flimsiest, and what little cogency they have is based upon the assumption noticed above that one of the two must have been an 'insidiator.' Argument no. 4 is practically disposed of by the statement of the Clodians, apparently true, that Clodius had a *bona fide* business engagement at Aricia. There might be some force in no. 6 if it were not that Milo's retinue appears to have been the more numerous.

β on the whole is proved, though it may be noticed that we hear incidentally of an argument adduced by the opponents which is not directly met by Cicero. The prosecutor laid stress upon the early hour at which Milo arrived at Bovillae and at which the fight took place, and argued apparently that Milo's movements showed a suspicious haste to anticipate Clodius' return. In the trial itself Cicero met this argument by a joke. When the prosecutor repeated the question "at what time was Clodius killed?" Cicero replied "sero," a *double entendre* between "late in the afternoon" and "too late[27];" in our speech he meets it by stating that the fight took place about 4 o'clock and describing Milo's movements as being throughout leisurely.

But while Cicero proves with tolerable certainty

---

[27] Quintil. vi. 3, 49, compare § 29 of the speech, where the words *hora fere undecima, aut non multo secus*, show a sense of weakness on Cicero's part.

that the fight was not of Milo's plotting, his labour is wasted. For the fact appears to be that Clodius was not killed in the skirmish but only wounded, that he took refuge in a tavern in Bovillae, was dragged out thence by Milo's order and murdered in cold blood; this appears to have been proved at the trial by the inhabitants of the place. As a matter of fact it was on this ground that Milo was condemned[28]. That Cicero should completely ignore it and indeed suggest exactly the contrary shows both how desperate his cause was and how little trust we can put in his statements in other cases. At the same time it shows us why he made so strong an effort to establish the suggestion, unproved but in itself natural enough, that Clodius waylaid Milo. Had this been the case, it would have palliated though hardly excused the cold-blooded murder.

There are two other important elements in the case. Milo after the murder was suspected vaguely of revolutionary plots like those of Catiline, and more definitely of a plot to murder Pompey. This charge, which according to Cicero told against Milo with the jury more than the murder itself, is only met indirectly and chiefly with declamation. The most definite piece of evidence against Milo was apparently the information laid by the 'sacrificulus' Licinius

---

[28] Asc. 32 *videbantur non ignorasse iudices, inscio Milone, vulneratum esse Clodium, sed compererant, postquam vulneratus esset, iussu Milonis occisum.*

that the slaves of Milo had confessed the existence of a plot. Cicero pooh-poohs the whole story but Milo's failure to produce the incriminated slaves must no doubt have told against him[29].

Finally it was open to Cicero to plead that the murder of a revolutionist was in itself a meritorious or at any rate a justifiable action. Such a plea would no doubt have found favour with a section of the jury. Cicero in fact was advised at the time[30] by many to adopt this course, and a speech embodying this plea was actually composed by Brutus[31]. In the existing speech the plea is disclaimed, but the disclaimer is only formal. The 'extra causam' sections in which a fierce invective is launched against Clodius are amongst the most effective of the speech. Quintilian rightly gives the speech as an instance of the plea 'non occidi, sed si occidi, recte feci[32].' It is not the least interesting part of the 'Milo' that it measures for us the extent to which political assassination could be justified at Rome. The advocate could hardly venture to plead that his client had committed a political murder and stopped short at saying that he would have had no scruple in doing so[33].

[29] Asc. on §67. Pompey sent word to Milo, *ut servos in potestate sua haberet*, i.e. not to sell or enfranchise them. Milo replied *ex iis servis quos nominasset, partim neminem se unquam habuisse, partim manumisisse.*

[30] Asc. §30.   [31] Asc. §30.   [32] Quint. iv. 5, 15.

[33] Cp. pro Rabir. § 18 *arguis occisum esse a C. Rabirio L. Saturninum. At id Rabirius multorum testimoniis antea falsum esse docuit. Ego autem si mihi esset integrum, susciperem hoc crimen, agnoscerem, confiterer.*

IV. The peroration has naturally but little argument and rests its claim upon its brilliant though surely unreal rhetoric. One point in it however requires notice. According to Plutarch[34], nothing damaged Milo's cause more than his dogged defiance and refusal to submit to the orthodox devices common amongst defendants for exciting pity. Cicero meets this very formidable difficulty with remarkable skill. While he goes as far as he consistently can, in ascribing a certain dignified pathos to Milo[35], he feels that this is not enough. The jury require the accused to humiliate himself, before they will acquit him. As Milo will not be humbled Cicero takes upon himself the humiliation, and asks for mercy for his client as a favour to himself.

The forensic merits of the 'Milo' are well summed up by Quintilian VI. 5, 10. "What is one most to admire in the 'Milo'? The orator's reservation of the 'narratio' till all the praejudicia are disposed of—his shifting the odium of 'insidiae' on to Clodius, though the conflict was in reality a chance affair—his avowed approval of the act, combined with a denial of intention on Milo's part—or his taking upon himself a suppliant attitude, which he could not ascribe to his client?"

[34] Cic. 35.
[35] Quint. VI. 1, 27 *Cicero quamquam preces non dat Milonis eumque potius animi praesentia commendat, accommodavit ei tamen verba, convenientes etiam forti viro conquestiones "o frustra mei suscepti labores" &c.*

6. *The original speech.*

Cicero did not break down at the trial as is sometimes said[36]. All that Asconius[37] says is 'Cicero cum inciperet dicere exceptus est acclamatione Clodianorum, qui se continere ne metu quidem circumstantium militum potuerunt. Itaque non ea qua solitus est constantia dixit.' Plutarch (Cic. 35) says even less, "he was confused and could hardly begin his speech: his body shook and the words stuck in his throat." But he does not seem to imply that the orator was unable to get through his speech in some fashion, and as the speech was complete enough to be taken down in shorthand and preserved at any rate till the time of Asconius it may safely be said that Dion Cassius XL. 54 is exaggerating when he says that Cicero retired after a few words[38].

As to the contents of the speech, the description given by a scholiast[39] is very much what we should expect, 'exstat alius praeterea liber actionis pro Milone, in quo omnia interrupta et impolita et rudia, plena denique maximi terroris agnoscas.' We have

---

[36] e.g. Froude's Caesar p. 346 'He stammered, blundered and sat down.'

[37] Asc. 31.

[38] ἐξεπλάγη καὶ κατέδεισεν, ὥστε τῶν μὲν παρεσκευασμένων μηδὲν εἰπεῖν, βραχὺ δέ τι καὶ τεθνηκὸς χαλεπῶς φθεγξάμενον ἀγαπητῶς μεταστῆναι.

[39] Schol. Bob. p. 276 (Orelli).

no known quotation from it, except one possible and important exception.

Quintilian IX. 2, 54 quotes without giving any reference as an instance of aposiopesis the following passage :

‘ An huius ille legis quam Clodius a se inventam gloriatur mentionem facere ausus esset vivo Milone, non dicam consule; de nostrum enim omnium—non audeo totum dicere.’   Again a scholiast on the lost ‘ De aere alieno Milonis’ has the following :

‘ Huius legis mentio fit in contione quae habita est pro Milone. Atque per [40]—(then a blank) de nostrorum omnium—non audeo totum dicere. Videte quid ea lex exitii | vitii | habitura fuerit cuius periculosa etiam reprehensio est.’

These two fragments overlap each other, and if they are pieced together we get the following :

‘ An huius legis quam Clodius a se inventam gloriatur mentionem facere ausus esset vivo Milone, non dicam consule : de nostrum enim omnium—non audeo totum dicere. Videte quid ea lex exitii habitura fuerit cuius periculosa etiam reprehensio est.’ Now it may be regarded as fairly certain that this is a fragment either from a lacuna in the existing speech for Milo, or from the lost speech. Peyron inserted it in § 33 of our speech between

---

[40] The words *atque per* probably belong to the scholiast, not to the quotation. Gaumitz filled up the blank with *tachygraphos excepta.*

'deferre posses' and 'et aspexit,' where it makes excellent sense. Many editors have followed him. Others still regard it as a fragment from the lost speech. So Müller and Nohl; and perhaps of late years the majority of scholars have inclined to this view. If they are right, it follows that the original speech was well known in Quintilian's time, for otherwise he would hardly have quoted it without some remark[41].

Apart from this we know that in the original, as in the existing speech, the exordium took the form of a digression[42] and that the whole argument was directed to proving that Clodius waylaid Milo[43]. Perhaps from this we may infer that the 'extra causam' sections (72—91), declaring that the murder was a meritorious action are an addition of the later speech. One other conjecture may, I think, be fairly made. If Cicero kept his temper at all, he would

[41] It is to be wished that editors who reject the proposed insertion into our speech would be more explicit in their reasons. Meanwhile there seems to me to be much force in Orelli's and Peyron's remarks. The *et aspexit* is much harsher without the insertion than with it. The passage, if it occurred in the first edition, would naturally have been worked into the second, and Quintilian would hardly quote from the original speech without some remark. It does not appear that apart from this fragment there is any certain evidence that Quintilian knew the original version. In iv. 3, 17 *unde Ciceroni quoque in prooemio cum diceret pro Milone, digredi fuit necesse, ut ipsa oratiuncula qua usus est, patet*, the word *oratiuncula* refers perhaps to the *commentarii* or short notes, which Cicero used in speaking and which were preserved and known to Quintilian (x. 7, 30).

[42] Quint. iv. 3, 17.

[43] *eo tota oratio eius spectavit*, Asc. 30.

surely adopt a conciliatory tone to Pompey, and the bitter tone of resentment, which, I believe, underlies the existing speech, would naturally find expression *after* the trial, when Cicero was both exasperated at the result and had ceased to feel the need of conciliation.

Of the date at which our present version was published we have no certain knowledge. But everything points to the conclusion that it was composed not long after the trial, while Cicero was still estranged from Pompey, while he was still smarting under his failure, and before he set out for Cilicia in the following year.

M. TULLI CICERONIS

PRO T. ANNIO MILONE

ORATIO AD IUDICES

I. Etsi vereor, iudices, ne turpe sit pro fortissimo **1**
viro dicere incipientem timere minimeque deceat, cum
T. Annius ipse magis de rei publicae salute quam de
sua perturbetur, me ad eius causam parem animi
magnitudinem afferre non posse, tamen haec novi
iudicii nova forma terret oculos, qui quocumque
inciderunt, consuetudinem fori et pristinum morem
iudiciorum requirunt. Non enim corona consessus
vester cinctus est, ut solebat, non usitata frequentia
stipati sumus, non illa praesidia, quae pro templis **2**
omnibus cernitis, etsi contra vim collocata sunt, non
afferunt tamen [oratori] aliquid, ut in foro et in
iudicio, quamquam praesidiis salutaribus et necessariis
saepti sumus, tamen ne non timere quidem sine aliquo
timore possimus. Quae si opposita Miloni putarem,
cederem tempori, iudices, nec inter tantam vim
armorum existimarem esse orationi locum. Sed me
recreat et reficit Cn. Pompei, sapientissimi et iustissimi viri, consilium, qui profecto nec iustitiae suae

putaret esse, quem reum sententiis iudicum tradidisset,
eundem telis militum dedere, nec sapientiae temeri-
tatem concitatae multitudinis auctoritate publica
3 armare. Quam ob rem illa arma, centuriones, cohortes
non periculum nobis, sed praesidium denuntiant,
neque solum ut quieto, sed etiam ut magno animo
simus hortantur neque auxilium modo defensioni
meae, verum etiam silentium pollicentur. Reliqua
vero multitudo, quae quidem est civium, tota nostra
est, neque eorum quisquam, quos undique intuentis,
unde aliqua fori pars aspici potest, et huius exitum
iudicii expectantis videtis, non cum virtuti Milonis
favet, tum de se, de liberis suis, de patria, de fortunis
hodierno die decertari putat. II. Unum genus est
adversum infestumque nobis eorum, quos P. Clodi
furor rapinis et incendiis et omnibus exitiis publicis
pavit ; qui hesterna etiam contione incitati sunt, ut
vobis voce praeirent, quid iudicaretis. Quorum
clamor si qui forte fuerit, admonere vos debebit, ut
eum civem retineatis, qui semper genus illud hominum
clamoresque maximos prae vestra salute neglexit.
4 Quam ob rem adeste animis, iudices, et timorem, si
quem habetis, deponite. Nam, si umquam de bonis
et fortibus viris, si umquam de bene meritis civibus
potestas vobis iudicandi fuit, si denique umquam
locus amplissimorum ordinum delectis viris datus est,
ut sua studia erga fortis et bonos civis, quae vultu et
verbis saepe significassent, re et sententiis declararent,
hoc profecto tempore eam potestatem omnem vos
habetis, ut statuatis, utrum nos, qui semper vestrae
auctoritati dediti fuimus, semper miseri lugeamus an
diu vexati a perditissimis civibus aliquando per vos

ac per vestram fidem, virtutem sapientiamque recre-
emur. Quid enim nobis duobus, iudices, laboriosius, **5**
quid magis sollicitum, magis exercitum dici aut fingi
potest, qui spe amplissimorum praemiorum ad rem
publicam adducti metu crudelissimorum suppliciorum
carere non possumus? Equidem ceteras tempestates
et procellas in illis dumtaxat fluctibus contionum
semper putavi Miloni esse subeundas, quia semper
pro bonis contra improbos senserat, in iudicio vero et
in eo consilio, in quo ex cunctis ordinibus amplissimi
viri iudicarent, numquam existimavi spem ullam esse
habituros Milonis inimicos ad eius non modo salutem
extinguendam, sed etiam gloriam per tales viros in-
fringendam. Quamquam in hac causa, iudices, T. **6**
Anni tribunatu rebusque omnibus pro salute rei
publicae gestis ad huius criminis defensionem non
abutemur. Nisi oculis videritis insidias Miloni a
Clodio factas, nec deprecaturi sumus, ut crimen hoc
nobis propter multa praeclara in rem publicam merita
condonetis, nec postulaturi, ut, si mors P. Clodi salus
vestra fuerit, idcirco eam virtuti Milonis potius quam
populi Romani felicitati assignetis. Sed si illius
insidiae clariores hac luce fuerint, tum denique obse-
crabo obtestaborque vos, iudices, si cetera amisimus,
hoc saltem nobis ut relinquatur, vitam ab inimicorum
audacia telisque ut inpune liceat defendere.

III. Sed antequam ad eam orationem venio, quae **7**
est propria vestrae quaestionis, videntur ea esse refu-
tanda, quae et in senatu ab inimicis saepe iactata
sunt et in contione ab improbis et paulo ante ab
accusatoribus, ut omni errore sublato rem plane, quae
veniat in iudicium, videre possitis. Negant intueri

lucem esse fas ei, qui a se hominem occisum esse
fateatur.   In qua tandem urbe hoc homines stultissimi
disputant?   Nempe in ea, quae primum iudicium de
capite vidit M. Horati, fortissimi viri, qui nondum
libera civitate tamen populi Romani comitiis liberatus
est, cum sua manu sororem esse interfectam fateretur.
8 An est quisquam, qui hoc ignoret, cum de homine
occiso quaeratur, aut negari solere omnino esse factum
aut recte et iure factum esse defendi?   Nisi vero
existimatis dementem P. Africanum fuisse, qui cum
a C. Carbone tribuno pl. seditiose in contione interro-
garetur, quid de Ti. Gracchi morte sentiret, respon-
derit iure caesum videri.   Neque enim posset aut
Ahala ille Servilius aut P. Nasica aut L. Opimius
aut C. Marius aut me consule senatus non nefarius
haberi, si sceleratos civis interfici nefas esset.   Itaque
hoc, iudices, non sine causa etiam fictis fabulis doctissimi homines memoriae prodiderunt, eum, qui
patris ulciscendi causa matrem necavisset, variatis
hominum sententiis non solum divina, sed etiam
9 sapientissimae deae sententia liberatum.   Quodsi
duodecim tabulae nocturnum furem quoquo modo,
diurnum autem, si se telo defenderet, interfici inpune
voluerunt, quis est, qui, quoquo modo quis interfectus
sit, puniendum putet, cum videat aliquando gladium
nobis ad hominem occidendum ab ipsis porrigi legibus?
IV.   Atqui, si tempus est ullum iure hominis necandi,
quae multa sunt, certe illud est non modo iustum,
verum etiam necessarium, cum vi vis illata defenditur.
Pudicitiam cum eriperet militi tribunus militaris in
exercitu C. Mari, propinquus eius imperatoris, interfectus ab eo est, cui vim afferebat.   Facere enim

probus adulescens periculose quam perpeti turpiter
maluit. Atque hunc ille summus vir scelere solutum
periculo liberavit. Insidiatori vero et latroni quae **10**
potest inferri iniusta nex? Quid comitatus nostri,
quid gladii volunt? quos habere certe non liceret, si
uti illis nullo pacto liceret. Est igitur haec, iudices,
non scripta, sed nata lex, quam non didicimus,
accepimus, legimus, verum ex natura ipsa arripuimus,
hausimus, expressimus, ad quam non docti, sed facti,
non instituti, sed imbuti sumus, ut, si vita nostra in
aliquas insidias, si in vim et in tela aut latronum aut
inimicorum incidisset, omnis honesta ratio esset expe-
diendae salutis. Silent enim leges inter arma nec se
expectari iubent, cum ei, qui expectare velit, ante
iniusta poena luenda sit quam iusta repetenda. Etsi **11**
persapienter et quodam modo tacite dat ipsa lex
potestatem defendendi, quae non modo hominem
occidi, sed esse cum telo hominis occidendi causa
vetat, ut, cum causa, non telum quaereretur, qui sui
defendendi causa telo esset usus, non hominis occidendi causa habuisse telum iudicaretur. Quapropter
hoc maneat in causa, iudices; non enim dubito, quin
probaturus sim vobis defensionem meam, si id memi-
neritis, quod oblivisci non potestis, insidiatorem iure
interfici posse.

V. Sequitur illud, quod a Milonis inimicis sae- **12**
pissime dicitur, caedem, in qua P. Clodius occisus est,
senatum iudicasse contra rem publicam esse factam.
Illam vero senatus non sententiis suis solum, sed
etiam studiis comprobavit. Quotiens enim est illa
causa a nobis acta in senatu quibus assensionibus uni-
versi ordinis, quam nec tacitis nec occultis! Quando

enim frequentissimo senatu quattuor aut summum
quinque sunt inventi, qui Milonis causam non pro-
barent? Declarant huius ambusti tribuni pl. illae
intermortuae contiones, quibus cotidie meam potentiam invidiose criminabatur, cum diceret senatum
non, quod sentiret, sed, quod ego vellem, decernere.
Quae quidem si potentia est appellanda potius quam
aut propter magna in rem publicam merita mediocris
in bonis causis auctoritas aut propter hos officiosos
labores meos non nulla apud bonos gratia, appelletur
ita sane, dum modo ea nos utamur pro salute bonorum
13 contra amentiam perditorum. Hanc vero quaestionem,
etsi non est iniqua, numquam tamen senatus con-
stituendam putavit. Erant enim leges, erant quaestiones vel de caede vel de vi, nec tantum maerorem
ac luctum senatui mors P. Clodi afferebat, ut nova
quaestio constitueretur. Cuius enim de illo incesto
stupro iudicium decernendi senatui potestas esset
erepta, de eius interitu quis potest credere senatum
iudicium novum constituendum putasse? Cur igitur
incendium curiae, oppugnationem aedium M. Lepidi,
caedem hanc ipsam contra rem publicam senatus
factam esse decrevit? Quia nulla vis umquam est in
libera civitate suscepta inter civis non contra rem
14 publicam. Non enim est illa defensio contra vim
umquam optanda, sed non numquam est necessaria;
nisi vero aut ille dies, quo Ti. Gracchus est caesus,
aut ille, quo Gaius, aut quo arma Saturnini [non],
etiamsi e re publica oppressa sunt, rem publicam
tamen non vulnerarunt. VI. Itaque ego ipse decrevi,
cum caedem in Appia factam esse constaret, non
eum, qui se defendisset, contra rem publicam fecisse,

sed, cum inesset in re vis et insidiae, crimen iudicio reservavi, rem notavi. Quodsi per furiosum illum tribunum senatui, quod sentiebat, perficere licuisset, novam quaestionem nullam haberemus. Decernebat enim, ut veteribus legibus tantum modo extra ordinem quaereretur. Divisa sententia est postulante nescio quo; nihil enim necesse est omnium me flagitia proferre. Sic reliqua auctoritas senatus empta intercessione sublata est.

At enim Cn. Pompeius rogatione sua et de re et **15** de causa iudicavit; tulit enim de caede, quae in Appia via facta esset, in qua P. Clodius occisus esset. Quid ergo tulit? Nempe ut quaereretur. Quid porro quaerendum est? factumne sit? At constat. A quo? At paret. Vidit igitur etiam in confessione facti iuris tamen defensionem suscipi posse. Quod nisi vidisset, posse absolvi eum, qui fateretur, cum videret nos fateri, neque quaeri umquam iussisset nec vobis tam hanc salutarem in iudicando litteram quam illam tristem dedisset. Mihi vero Cn. Pompeius non modo nihil gravius contra Milonem iudicasse, sed etiam statuisse videtur, quid vos in iudicando spectare oporteret. Nam, qui non poenam confessioni, sed defensionem dedit, is causam interitus quaerendam, non interitum putavit. Iam illud ipse dicet profecto, **16** quod sua sponte fecit, Publione Clodio tribuendum putarit an tempori. VII. Domi suae nobilissimus vir senatus propugnator atque illis quidem temporibus paene patronus, avunculus huius iudicis nostri fortissimi viri, M. Catonis, tribunus pl. M. Drusus occisus est. Nihil de eius morte populus consultus, nulla quaestio decreta a senatu est. Quantum luctum in

hac urbe fuisse a nostris patribus accepimus, cum P.
Africano domi suae quiescenti illa nocturna vis esset
illata! Quis tum non gemuit, quis non arsit dolore,
quem inmortalem, si fieri posset, omnes esse cuperent,
eius ne necessariam quidem expectatam esse mortem?
Num igitur ulla quaestio de Africani morte lata est?
17 Certe nulla. Quid ita? Quia non alio facinore clari
homines, alio obscuri necantur. Intersit inter vitae
dignitatem summorum atque infimorum; mors quidem
inlata per scelus isdem et poenis teneatur et legibus.
Nisi forte magis erit parricida, si qui consularem
patrem quam si quis humilem necarit, aut eo mors
atrocior erit P. Clodi, quod is in monumentis maiorum
suorum sit interfectus; hoc enim ab istis saepe
dicitur; proinde quasi Appius ille Caecus viam muni-
verit, non qua populus uteretur, sed ubi inpune sui
18 posteri latrocinarentur! Itaque in eadem ista Appia
via cum ornatissimum equitem Romanum P. Clodius,
M. Papirium, occidisset, non fuit illud facinus puniendum (homo enim nobilis in suis monumentis equitem
Romanum occiderat); nunc eiusdem Appiae nomen
quantas tragoedias excitat! Quae cruentata antea
caede honesti atque innocentis viri silebatur, eadem
nunc crebro usurpatur, posteaquam latronis et parricidae sanguine imbuta est. Sed quid ego illa com-
memoro? Comprehensus est in templo Castoris servus
P. Clodi, quem ille ad Cn. Pompeium interficiendum
collocarat. Extorta est ei confitenti sica de manibus.
Caruit foro postea Pompeius, caruit senatu, caruit
publico; ianua se ac parietibus, non iure legum
19 iudiciorumque texit. Num quae rogatio lata, num
quae nova quaestio decreta est? Atqui, si res, si vir,

si tempus ullum dignum fuit, certe haec in illa causa summa omnia fuerunt. Insidiator erat in foro collocatus atque in vestibulo ipso senatus, ei viro autem mors parabatur, cuius in vita nitebatur salus civitatis, eo porro rei publicae tempore, quo si unus ille cecidisset, non haec solum civitas, sed gentes omnes concidissent. Nisi vero, quia perfecta res non est, non fuit punienda; proinde quasi exitus rerum, non hominum consilia legibus vindicentur. Minus dolendum fuit re non perfecta, sed puniendum certe nihilo minus. Quotiens ego ipse, iudices, ex P. Clodi telis **20** et ex cruentis eius manibus effugi! ex quibus si me non vel mea vel rei publicae fortuna servasset, quis tandem de interitu meo quaestionem tulisset?

VIII. Sed stulti sumus, qui Drusum, qui Africanum, Pompeium, nosmet ipsos cum P. Clodio conferre audeamus. Tolerabilia fuerunt illa; P. Clodi mortem aequo animo ferre nemo potest; luget senatus, maeret equester ordo, tota civitas confecta senio est, squalent municipia, afflictantur coloniae, agri denique ipsi tam beneficum, tam salutarem, tam mansuetum civem desiderant. Non fuit ea causa, iudices, profecto, non **21** fuit, cur sibi censeret Pompeius quaestionem ferendam, sed homo sapiens atque alta et divina quadam mente praeditus multa vidit: fuisse illum sibi inimicum, familiarem Milonem; in communi omnium laetitia si etiam ipse gauderet, timuit, ne videretur infirmior fides reconciliatae gratiae. Multa etiam alia vidit, sed illud maxime, quamvis atrociter ipse tulisset, vos tamen fortiter iudicaturos. Itaque delegit ex florentissimis ordinibus ipsa lumina, neque vero, quod non nulli dictitant, secrevit in iudicibus

legendis amicos meos.   Neque enim hoc cogitavit vir
iustissimus neque in bonis viris legendis id assequi
potuisset, etiamsi cupisset.   Non enim mea gratia
familiaritatibus continetur, quae late patere non
possunt, propterea quod consuetudines victus non
possunt esse cum multis; sed, si quid possumus, ex
eo possumus, quod res publica nos coniunxit cum
bonis.   Ex quibus ille cum optimos viros legeret
idque maxime ad fidem suam pertinere arbitraretur,
22 non potuit legere non studiosos mei.   Quod vero te,
L. Domiti, huic quaestioni praeesse maxime voluit,
nihil quaesivit aliud nisi iustitiam, gravitatem, huma-
nitatem, fidem.   Tulit, ut consularem necesse esset,
credo, quod principum munus esse ducebat resistere
et levitati multitudinis et perditorum temeritati.
Ex consularibus te creavit potissimum; dederas enim,
quam contemneres populares insanias, iam ab adulescentia documenta maxima.

23   IX.   Quam ob rem, iudices, ut aliquando ad
causam crimenque veniamus, si neque omnis confessio
facti est inusitata neque de causa nostra quicquam
aliter, ac nos vellemus, a senatu iudicatum est et
lator ipse legis, cum esset controversia nulla facti,
iuris tamen disceptationem esse voluit et ei lecti
iudices isque praepositus *est* quaestioni, qui haec iuste
sapienterque disceptet, reliquum est, iudices, ut nihil
iam quaerere aliud debeatis, nisi uter utri insidias
fecerit.   Quod quo facilius argumentis perspicere
possitis, rem gestam vobis dum breviter expono,
quaeso, diligenter attendite.

24   P. Clodius cum statuisset omni scelere in praetura vexare rem publicam videretque ita tracta

esse comitia anno superiore, ut non multos menses
praeturam gerere posset, qui non honoris gradum
spectaret ut ceteri, sed et L. Paulum collegam
effugere vellet, singulari virtute civem, et annum
integrum ad dilacerandam rem publicam quaereret,
subito reliquit annum suum seseque in annum proxi-
mum transtulit non, ut fit, religione aliqua, sed ut
haberet, quod ipse dicebat, ad praeturam gerendam,
hoc est ad evertendam rem publicam, plenum annum
atque integrum. Occurrebat ei mancam ac debilem 25
praeturam futuram suam consule Milone ; eum porro
summo consensu populi Romani consulem fieri videbat. Contulit se ad eius conpetitores, sed ita, totam
ut petitionem ipse solus etiam invitis illis gubernaret,
tota ut comitia suis, ut dictitabat, umeris sustineret.
Convocabat tribus, se interponebat, Collinam novam
dilectu perditissimorum civium conscribebat. Quanto
ille plura miscebat, tanto hic magis in dies convalescebat. Ubi vidit homo ad omne facinus paratissimus
fortissimum virum inimicissimum suum certissimum
consulem idque intellexit non solum sermonibus, sed
etiam suffragiis populi Romani saepe esse declaratum,
palam agere coepit et aperte dicere occidendum
Milonem. Servos agrestes et barbaros, quibus silvas 26
publicas depopulatus erat Etruriamque vexarat, ex
Appennino deduxerat, quos videbatis. Res erat
minime obscura. Etenim palam dictitabat consulatum Miloni eripi non posse, vitam posse. Signifi-
cavit hoc saepe in senatu, dixit in contione ; quin
etiam M. Favonio, fortissimo viro, quaerenti ex eo,
qua spe fureret Milone vivo, respondit triduo illum
aut summum quadriduo esse periturum ; quam vocem

eius ad hunc M. Catonem statim Favonius detulit.

27 X.   Interim cum sciret Clodius (neque enim erat difficile id scire) iter sollemne, legitimum, necessarium ante diem XIII Kalendas Februarias Miloni esse Lanuvium ad flaminem prodendum, quod erat dictator Lanuvi Milo, Roma subito ipse profectus pridie est, ut ante suum fundum, quod re intellectum est, Miloni insidias collocaret, atque ita profectus est, ut contionem turbulentam, in qua eius furor desideratus est, quae illo ipso die habita est, relinqueret, quam, nisi obire facinoris locum tempusque voluisset, num-

28 quam reliquisset.   Milo autem cum in senatu fuisset eo die, quoad senatus est dimissus, domum venit, calceos et vestimenta mutavit, paulisper, dum se uxor, ut fit, comparat, commoratus est, dein profectus id temporis, cum iam Clodius, siquidem eo die Romam venturus erat, redire potuisset.   Obviam fit ei Clodius expeditus, in equo, nulla raeda, nullis inpedimentis, nullis Graecis comitibus, ut solebat, sine uxore, quod numquam fere, cum hic insidiator, qui iter illud ad caedem faciendam apparasset, cum uxore veheretur in raeda, paenulatus, magno et impedito et muliebri

29 ac delicato ancillarum puerorumque comitatu. Fit obviam Clodio ante fundum eius hora fere undecima aut non multo secus.   Statim conplures cum telis in hunc faciunt de loco superiore impetum adversi, raedarium occidunt.   Cum autem hic de raeda reiecta paenula desiluisset seque acri animo defenderet, illi, qui erant cum Clodio, gladiis eductis partim recurrere ad raedam, ut a tergo Milonem adorirentur, partim, quod hunc iam interfectum putarent, caedere incipiunt eius servos, qui post erant; ex quibus qui animo

fideli in dominum et praesenti fuerunt, partim occisi
sunt, partim, cum ad raedam pugnari viderent,
domino succurrere prohiberentur, Milonem occisum
et ex ipso Clodio audirent et re vera putarent,
fecerunt id servi Milonis (dicam enim aperte non
derivandi criminis causa, sed ut factum est) nec
imperante nec sciente nec praesente domino, quod
suos quisque servos in tali re facere voluisset.

XI. Haec, sicuti exposui, ita gesta sunt, iudices; 30
insidiator superatus est, vi victa vis vel potius
oppressa virtute audacia est. Nihil dico, quid res
publica consecuta sit, nihil, quid vos, nihil, quid
omnes boni; nihil sane id prosit Miloni, qui hoc fato
natus est, ut ne se quidem servare potuerit, quin una
rem publicam vosque servaret. Si id iure fieri non
potuit, nihil habeo, quod defendam. Sin hoc et
ratio doctis et necessitas barbaris et mos gentibus et
feris etiam beluis natura ipsa praescripsit, ut omnem
semper vim, quacumque ope possent, a corpore, a
capite, a vita sua propulsarent, non potestis hoc
facinus improbum iudicare, quin simul iudicetis
omnibus, qui in latrones inciderint, aut illorum telis
aut vestris sententiis esse pereundum. Quod si ita 31
putasset, certe optabilius Miloni fuit dare iugulum
P. Clodio non semel ab illo neque tum primum
petitum quam iugulari a vobis, quia se non iugu-
landum illi tradidisset. Sin hoc nemo vestrum ita
sentit, non illud iam in iudicium venit, occisusne sit,
quod fatemur, sed iure an iniuria, quod multis in
causis saepe quaesitum est. Insidias factas esse
constat, et id est, quod senatus contra rem publicam
factum iudicavit; ab utro factae sint, incertum est.

De hoc igitur latum est ut quaereretur.   Ita et
senatus rem, non hominem notavit, et Pompeius de
iure, non de facto quaestionem tulit.   XII. Num
quid igitur aliud in iudicium venit, nisi uter utri
insidias fecerit?   Profecto nihil; si hic illi, ut ne sit
inpune, si ille huic, ut scelere solvamur.

32   Quonam igitur pacto probari potest insidias Miloni
fecisse Clodium?   Satis est in illa quidem tam audaci,
tam nefaria belua docere magnam ei causam, magnam
spem in Milonis morte propositam, magnas utilitates
fuisse.   Itaque illud Cassianum, 'cui bono' fuerit,
in his personis valeat, etsi boni nullo emolumento
impelluntur in fraudem, improbi saepe parvo.   Atqui
Milone interfecto Clodius haec assequebatur, non
modo ut praetor esset non eo consule, quo sceleris
nihil facere posset, sed etiam ut iis consulibus praetor
esset, quibus si non adiuvantibus, at coniventibus
certe speraret se posse eludere in illis suis cogitatis
furoribus; cuius illi conatus, ut ipse ratiocinabatur,
nec cuperent reprimere, si possent, cum tantum
beneficium ei se debere arbitrarentur, et, si vellent,
fortasse vix possent frangere hominis sceleratissimi
33 corroboratam iam vetustate audaciam.   An vero,
iudices, vos soli ignoratis, vos hospites in hac urbe
versamini, vestrae peregrinantur aures neque in hoc
pervagato civitatis sermone versantur, quas ille leges,
si leges nominandae sunt ac non faces urbis, pestes
rei publicae, fuerit impositurus nobis omnibus atque
inusturus?   Exhibe, quaeso, Sexte Clodi, exhibe
librarium illud legum vestrarum, quod te aiunt
eripuisse e domo et ex mediis armis turbaque
nocturna tamquam Palladium extulisse, ut prae-

clarum videlicet munus atque instrumentum tribunatus ad aliquem, si nactus esses, qui tuo arbitrio
tribunatum gereret, deferre posses. Et aspexit me
illis quidem oculis, quibus tum solebat, cum omnibus
omnia minabatur. Movet me quippe lumen curiae.
XIII. Quid? tu me tibi iratum, Sexte, putas, cuius
tu inimicissimum multo crudelius etiam punitus es,
quam erat humanitatis meae postulare? Tu P. Clodi
cruentum cadaver eiecisti domo, tu in publicum
abiecisti, tu spoliatum imaginibus, exequiis, pompa,
laudatione, infelicissimis lignis semustilatum nocturnis
canibus dilaniandum reliquisti. Quare, etsi nefarie
fecisti, tamen, quoniam in meo inimico crudelitatem
expromsisti tuam, laudare non possum, irasci certe
non debeo.***

*Audistis, iudices, quantum Clodi inter*fuerit occidi 34
Milonem; convertite animos nunc vicissim ad Milonem. Quid Milonis intererat interfici Clodium? quid
erat, cur Milo non dicam admitteret, sed optaret?
'Obstabat in spe consulatus Miloni Clodius.' At eo
repugnante fiebat, immo vero eo fiebat magis, nec me
suffragatore meliore utebatur quam Clodio. Valebat
apud vos, iudices, Milonis erga me remque publicam
meritorum memoria, valebant preces et lacrimae
nostrae, quibus ego tum vos mirifice moveri sen-
tiebam, sed plus multo valebat periculorum inpen-
dentium timor. Quis enim erat civium, qui sibi
solutam P. Clodi praeturam sine maximo rerum
novarum metu proponeret? Solutam autem fore
videbatis, nisi esset is consul, qui eam auderet posset-
que constringere. Eum Milonem unum esse cum
sentiret universus populus Romanus, quis dubitaret

suffragio suo se metu, periculo rem publicam liberare ?
At nunc, Clodio remoto, usitatis iam rebus enitendum
est Miloni, ut tueatur dignitatem suam ; singularis
illa et huic uni concessa gloria, quae cottidie augebatur frangendis furoribus Clodianis, iam Clodi morte
cecidit.   Vos adepti estis, ne quem civem metueretis ;
hic exercitationem virtutis, suffragationem consulatus,
fontem perennem gloriae suae perdidit.   Itaque
Milonis consulatus, qui vivo Clodio labefactari non
poterat, mortuo denique temptari coeptus est.   Non
modo igitur nihil prodest, sed obest etiam Clodi mors
35 Miloni.   'At valuit odium, fecit iratus, fecit inimicus,
fuit ultor iniuriae, punitor doloris sui.'   Quid ? si
haec non dico maiora fuerunt in Clodio quam in
Milone, sed in illo maxima, nulla in hoc, quid voltis
amplius ?   Quid enim odisset Clodium Milo, segetem
ac materiem suae gloriae, praeter hoc civile odium,
quo omnes inprobos odimus ?   Ille erat ut odisset
primum defensorem salutis meae, deinde vexatorem
furoris, domitorem armorum suorum, postremo etiam
accusatorem suum ; reus enim Milonis lege Plotia
fuit Clodius, quoad vixit.   Quo tandem animo hoc
tyrannum illum tulisse creditis ? quantum odium
illius et in homine iniusto quam etiam iustum fuisse ?
36   XIV.   Reliquum est, ut iam illum natura ipsius
consuetudoque defendat, hunc autem haec eadem
coarguant.   'Nihil per vim umquam Clodius, omnia
per vim Milo.'   Quid ? ego, iudices, cum maerentibus
vobis urbe cessi, iudiciumne timui, non servos, non
arma, non vim ?   Quae fuisset igitur iusta causa
restituendi mei, nisi fuisset iniusta eiciendi ?   Diem
mihi, credo, dixerat, multam irrogarat, actionem

perduellionis intenderat, et mihi videlicet in causa
aut mala aut mea, non et praeclarissima et vestra,
iudicium timendum fuit. Servorum et egentium
civium et facinerosorum armis meos cives meis consiliis periculisque servatos pro me obici nolui. Vidi **37**
enim, vidi hunc ipsum Q. Hortensium, lumen et
ornamentum rei publicae, paene interfici servorum
manu, cum mihi adesset; qua in turba C. Vibienus
senator, vir optimus, cum hoc cum esset una, ita est
mulcatus, ut vitam amiserit. Itaque quando illius
postea sica illa, quam a Catilina acceperat, conquievit? Haec intentata nobis est, huic ego vos obici
pro me non sum passus, haec insidiata Pompeio est,
haec istam Appiam, monumentum sui nominis, nece
Papiri cruentavit, haec eadem longo intervallo conversa rursus est in me; nuper quidem, ut scitis, me
ad regiam paene confecit. Quid simile Milonis? **38**
cuius vis omnis haec semper fuit, ne P. Clodius, cum
in iudicium detrahi non posset, vi oppressam civitatem teneret. Quem si interficere voluisset, quantae
quotiens occasiones, quam praeclarae fuerunt! Potuitne, cum domum ac deos penates suos illo oppug-
nante defenderet, iure se ulcisci, potuitne civi egregio
et viro fortissimo, P. Sestio, collega suo, vulnerato,
potuitne Q. Fabricio, viro optimo, cum de reditu meo
legem ferret, pulso, crudelissima in foro caede facta,
potuitne L. Caecili, iustissimi fortissimique praetoris,
oppugnata domo, potuitne illo die, cum est lata lex
de me, cum totius Italiae concursus, quem mea salus
concitarat, facti illius gloriam lubens agnovisset, ut,
etiamsi id Milo fecisset, cuncta civitas eam laudem
pro sua vindicaret? XV. At quod erat tempus!

39 Clarissimus et fortissimus consul inimicus Clodio, P.
Lentulus, ultor sceleris illius, propugnator senatus,
defensor vestrae voluntatis, patronus publici consen-
sus, restitutor salutis meae, septem praetores, octo
tribuni plebei illius adversarii, defensores mei, Cn.
Pompeius auctor et dux mei reditus, illius hostis,
cuius sententiam senatus omnis de salute mea gravissimam et ornatissimam secutus est, qui populum
Romanum est cohortatus, qui cum de me decretum
Capuae fecit, ipse cunctae Italiae cupienti et eius
fidem imploranti signum dedit, ut ad me restituendum
Romam concurrerent; omnium denique in illum odia
civium ardebant desiderio mei, quem qui tum interemisset, non de impunitate eius, sed de praemiis
40 cogitaretur.   Tamen se Milo continuit et P. Clodium
in iudicium bis, ad vim numquam vocavit.   Quid?
privato Milone et reo ad populum accusante P.
Clodio, cum in Cn. Pompeium pro Milone dicentem
impetus factus est, quae tum non modo occasio, sed
etiam causa illius opprimendi fuit!   Nuper vero cum
M. Antonius summam spem salutis bonis omnibus
attulisset gravissimamque adulescens nobilissimus rei
publicae partem fortissime suscepisset atque illam
beluam iudicii laqueos declinantem iam inretitam
teneret, qui locus, quod tempus illud, di immortales,
fuit! cum se ille fugiens in scalarum tenebras abdi-
disset, magnum Miloni fuit conficere illam pestem
nulla sua invidia, M. vero Antoni maxima gloria!
41 Quid? comitiis in campo quotiens potestas fuit, cum
ille in saepta ruisset, gladios destringendos, lapides
iaciendos curavisset, dein subito vultu Milonis per-
territus fugeret ad Tiberim, vos et omnes boni vota
faceretis ut Miloni uti virtute sua liberet!

XVI.   Quem igitur cum omnium gratia noluit, hunc voluit cum aliquorum querella, quem iure, quem loco, quem tempore, quem inpune non est ausus, hunc iniuria, iniquo loco, alieno tempore, periculo capitis non dubitavit occidere? praesertim, iudices, cum 42 honoris amplissimi contentio et dies comitiorum subesset, quo quidem tempore (scio enim, quam timida sit ambitio, quantaque et quam sollicita sit cupiditas consulatus) omnia, non modo quae reprehendi palam, sed etiam obscure quae cogitari possunt, timemus, rumorem, fabulam falsam, fictam, levem perhorrescimus, ora omnium atque oculos intuemur Nihil enim est tam molle, tam tenerum, tam aut fragile aut flexibile quam voluntas erga nos sensusque civium, qui non modo improbitati irascuntur candidatorum, sed etiam in recte factis saepe fastidiunt. Hunc diem igitur campi speratum atque exoptatum 43 sibi proponens Milo cruentis manibus scelus et facinus prae se ferens et confitens ad illa augusta centuriarum auspicia veniebat? Quam hoc non credibile in hoc, quam idem in Clodio non dubitandum, cum se ille interfecto Milone regnaturum putaret! Quid? quod caput est audaciae, iudices, quis ignorat maximam illecebram esse peccandi impunitatis spem? In utro igitur haec fuit? in Milone, qui etiam nunc reus est facti aut praeclari aut certe necessarii, an in Clodio, qui ita iudicia poenamque contempserat, ut eum nihil delectaret, quod aut per naturam fas esset aut per leges liceret?

Sed quid ego argumentor, quid plura disputo? 44 Te, Q. Petili, appello, optimum et fortissimum civem, te, M. Cato, testor. quos mihi divina quaedam sors

dedit iudices.   Vos ex M. Favonio audistis Clodium
sibi dixisse, et audistis vivo Clodio, periturum Milonem triduo; post diem tertium gesta res est, quam
dixerat.   Cum ille non dubitarit aperire, quid cogi-
45 tarit, vos potestis dubitare, quid fecerit?   XVII. Quem
ad modum igitur eum dies non fefellit?   Dixi equidem
modo.   Dictatoris Lanuvini stata sacrificia nosse
negotii nihil erat.   Vidit necesse esse Miloni proficisci Lanuvium illo ipso, quo est profectus, die,
itaque antevertit.   At quo die?   Quo, ut ante dixi,
fuit insanissima contio ab ipsius mercennario tribuno
pl. concitata; quem diem ille, quam contionem, quos
clamores, nisi ad cogitatum facinus adproperaret,
numquam reliquisset.   Ergo illi ne causa quidem
itineris, etiam causa manendi, Miloni manendi nulla
facultas, exeundi non causa solum, sed etiam necessitas fuit.   Quid, si, ut ille scivit Milonem fore eo
die in via, sic Clodium Milo ne suspicari quidem
46 potuit?   Primum quaero, qui id scire potuerit, quod
vos idem in Clodio quaerere non potestis.   Ut enim
neminem alium nisi T. Patinam, familiarissimum
suum, rogasset, scire potuit illo ipso die Lanuvi a
dictatore Milone prodi flaminem necesse esse.   Sed
erant permulti alii, ex quibus id facillime scire posset
[omnes scilicet Lanuvini].   Milo de Clodi reditu
unde quaesivit?   Quaesierit sane (videte, quid vobis
largiar), servum etiam, ut Q. Arrius, meus amicus,
dixit, corruperit.   Legite testimonia testium vestrorum.   Dixit C. Causinius Schola Interamnas, familiarissimus et idem comes Clodi, cuius iam pridem
testimonio Clodius eadem hora Interamnae fuerat et
Romae, P. Clodium illo die in Albano mansurum

fuisse, sed subito ei esse nuntiatum Cyrum archi-
tectum esse mortuum, itaque repente Romam con-
stituisse proficisci. Dixit hoc comes item P. Clodi,
C. Clodius. XVIII. Videte, iudices, quantae res 47
his testimoniis sint confectae. Primum certe liberatur
Milo non eo consilio profectus esse, ut insidiaretur in
via Clodio, quippe, si ille obvius ei futurus omnino
non erat. Deinde (non enim video, cur non meum
quoque agam negotium) scitis, iudices, fuisse, qui in
hac rogatione suadenda dicerent Milonis manu caedem
esse factam, consilio vero maioris alicuius. Me
videlicet latronem ac sicarium abiecti homines et
perditi describebant. Iacent suis testibus [ii], qui
Clodium negant eo die Romam, nisi de Cyro audisset,
fuisse rediturum. Respiravi, liberatus sum; non
vereor, ne, quod ne suspicari quidem potuerim, videar
id cogitasse. Nunc persequar cetera. Nam occurrit 48
illud: 'Igitur ne Clodius quidem de insidiis cogitavit,
quoniam fuit in Albano mansurus.' Si quidem exiturus ad caedem e villa non fuisset. Video enim
illum, qui dicatur de Cyri morte nuntiasse, non id
nuntiasse, sed Milonem appropinquare. Nam quid
de Cyro nuntiaret, quem Clodius Roma proficiscens
reliquerat morientem? Una fui, testamentum simul
obsignavi [cum Clodio]; testamentum autem palam
fecerat et illum heredem et me scripserat. Quem
pridie hora tertia animam efflantem reliquisset, eum
mortuum postridie hora decima denique ei nuntiabatur? XIX. Age, sit ita factum; quae causa, cur 49
Romam properaret, cur in noctem se coniceret? Ecquid afferebat festinationis, quod heres erat? Primum
erat nihil, cur properato opus esset; deinde, si quid

esset, quid tandem erat, quod ea nocte consequi
posset, amitteret autem, si postridie Romam mane
venisset? Atque ut illi nocturnus ad urbem adventus
vitandus potius quam expetendus fuit, sic Miloni,
cum insidiator esset, si illum ad urbem nocte accessurum sciebat, subsidendum atque exspectandum
50 fuit. Nemo ei neganti non credidisset, quem esse
omnes salvum etiam confitentem volunt. Sustinuisset
hoc crimen primum ipse ille latronum occultator et
receptor locus, cum neque muta solitudo indicasset
neque caeca nox ostendisset Milonem; deinde ibi
multi ab illo violati, spoliati, bonis expulsi, multi
haec etiam timentes in suspicionem caderent, tota
51 denique rea citaretur Etruria. Atqui illo die certe
Aricia rediens devertit Clodius ad Albanum. Quod
ut sciret Milo, illum Ariciae fuisse, suspicari tamen
debuit eum, etiamsi Romam illo die reverti vellet, ad
villam suam, quae viam tangeret, deversurum. Cur
neque ante occurrit, ne ille in villa resideret, nec eo
in loco subsedit, quo ille noctu venturus esset?

[Video adhuc constare, iudices, omnia, Miloni
etiam utile fuisse Clodium vivere, illi ad ea, quae
concupierat, optatissimum interitum Milonis; odium
fuisse illius in hunc acerbissimum, nullum huius in
illum; consuetudinem illius perpetuam in vi inferenda,
52 huius tantum in repellenda; mortem ab illo denun-
tiatam Miloni et praedictam palam, nihil umquam
auditum ex Milone; profectionis huius diem illi
notum, reditus illius huic ignotum fuisse; huius iter
necessarium, illius etiam potius alienum; hunc prae
se tulisse illo die Roma exiturum, illum eo die se
dissimulasse rediturum; hunc nullius rei mutasse

consilium, illum causam mutandi consilii finxisse ;
huic, si insidiaretur, noctem prope urbem expectandam,
illi, etiamsi hunc non timeret, tamen accessum ad
urbem nocturnum fuisse metuendum.

XX.   Videamus nunc id, quod caput est, locus 53
ad insidias ille ipse, ubi congressi sunt, utri tandem
fuerit aptior.   Id vero, iudices, etiam dubitandum et
diutius cogitandum est.   Ante fundum Clodi, quo in
fundo propter insanas illas substructiones facile hominum mille versabantur valentium, edito adversarii
atque excelso loco superiorem se fore putarat Milo
et ob eam rem eum locum ad pugnam potissimum
elegerat an in eo loco est potius expectatus ab eo, qui
ipsius loci spe facere impetum cogitarat?   Res loquitur ipsa, iudices, quae semper valet plurimum.   Si 54
haec non gesta audiretis, sed picta videretis, tamen
appareret, uter esset insidiator, uter nihil cogitaret
mali, cum alter veheretur in raeda paenulatus, una
sederet uxor.—Quid horum non inpeditissimum,
vestitus an vehiculum an comes? quid minus promptum ad pugnam, cum paenula inretitus, raeda inpe-
ditus, uxore paene constrictus esset?   Videte nunc
illum primum egredientem e villa subito (cur?),
vesperi (quid necesse est?), tarde (qui convenit, praesertim id temporis?).   'Devertit in villam Pompei.'
Pompeium ut videret?   Sciebat in Alsiensi esse.
Villam ut perspiceret?   Miliens in ea fuerat.   Quid
ergo erat?   Morae et tergiversationes ; dum hic veniret, locum relinquere noluit.

XXI.   Age nunc iter expediti latronis cum 55
Milonis inpedimentis comparate.   Semper ille antea
cum uxore, tum sine ea ; numquam nisi in raeda, tum

in equo; comites Graeculi, quocumque ibat, etiam
cum in castra Etrusca properabat, tum nugarum in
comitatu nihil.   Milo, qui numquam, tum casu pueros
symphoniacos uxoris ducebat et ancillarum greges.
Ille, qui semper secum scorta, semper exoletos, semper
lupas duceret, tum neminem, nisi ut (virum a viro
lectum) esse diceres.   Cur igitur victus est? Quia
non semper viator a latrone, non numquam etiam
latro a viatore occiditur ; quia, quamquam paratus in
imparatos [Clodius], (tamen mulier) inciderat in viros.

56 Nec vero sic erat umquam non paratus Milo contra
illum, ut non satis fere esset paratus.   Semper [ille],
et quantum interesset P. Clodi se perire, et quanto
illi odio esset, et quantum ille auderet, cogitabat.
Quam ob rem vitam suam, quam maximis praemiis
propositam et paene addictam sciebat, numquam in
periculum sine praesidio et sine custodia proiciebat.
Adde casus, adde incertos exitus pugnarum Martemque communem, qui saepe spoliantem iam et
exultantem evertit et perculit ab abiecto, adde in-
scitiam pransi, poti, oscitantis ducis, qui cum a tergo
hostem interclusum reliquisset, nihil de eius extremis
comitibus cogitavit, in quos incensos ira vitamque
domini desperantis cum incidisset, haesit in iis poenis,
quas ab eo servi fideles pro domini vita expetiverunt.

57 Cur igitur eos manu misit? Metuebat scilicet, ne
indicaretur, ne dolorem perferre non possent, ne
tormentis cogerentur occisum esse a servis Milonis
in Appia via P. Clodium confiteri.   Quid opus est
tortore? quid quaeris? occideritne? Occidit.   Iure
an iniuria?   Nihil ad tortorem ; facti enim in eculeo
quaestio est, iuris in iudicio.   XXII. Quod igitur

in causa quaerendum est, id agamus hic ; quod tormentis invenire vis, id fatemur. Manu vero cur
miserit, si id potius quaeris, quam cur parum amplis
affecerit praemiis, nescis inimici factum reprehendere.
Dixit enim hic idem, qui omnia semper constanter et 58
fortiter, M. Cato, et dixit in turbulenta contione,
quae tamen huius auctoritate placata est, non liber-
tate solum, sed etiam omnibus praemiis dignissimos
fuisse, qui domini caput defendissent. Quod enim
praemium satis magnum est tam benevolis, tam bonis,
tam fidelibus servis, propter quos vivit ? Etsi id
quidem non tanti est, quam quod propter eosdem non
sanguine et vulneribus suis crudelissimi inimici mentem oculosque satiavit. Quos nisi manu misisset,
tormentis etiam dedendi fuerunt conservatores domini,
ultores sceleris, defensores necis. Hic vero nihil
habet in his malis, quod minus moleste ferat, quam,
etiamsi quid ipsi accidat, esse tamen illis meritum
praemium persolutum. Sed quaestiones urgent Milo- 59
nem, quae sunt habitae nunc in atrio Libertatis.
Quibusnam de servis ? Rogas ? de P. Clodi. Quis
eos postulavit ? Appius. Quis produxit ? Appius.
Unde ? Ab Appio. Di boni ! quid potest agi severius ? De servis nulla lege quaestio est in dominum
nisi de incestu (ut fuit in Clodium. Proxime deos
accessit Clodius, propius quam tum, cum ad ipsos
penetrarat ; cuius de morte tamquam de caerimoniis
violatis quaeritur)—sed tamen maiores nostri in
dominum de servo quaeri noluerunt, non quin posset
verum inveniri, sed quia videbatur indignum esse et
domini morte ipsa tristius ; in reum de servo accusa-
toris cum quaeritur, verum inveniri potest ? Age 60

vero, quae erat aut qualis quaestio? 'Heus tu,
colloquim Rufio,' verbi causa, 'cave sis mentiare.(s) Clodius
insidias fecit Miloni?' 'Fecit.' Certa crux. 'Nullas
fecit.' Sperata libertas. Quid hac quaestione certius? Subito abrepti in quaestionem tamen separan-
tur a ceteris et in arcas coniciuntur, ne quis cum iis
colloqui possit. Hi centum dies penes accusatorem
cum fuissent, ab eo ipso accusatore producti sunt.
Quid hac quaestione dici potest integrius, quid incorruptius?

61   XXIII. Quodsi nondum satis cernitis, cum res
ipsa tot tam claris argumentis signisque luceat, pura
mente atque integra Milonem nullo scelere imbutum,
nullo metu perterritum, nulla conscientia exanimatum
Romam revertisse, recordamini, per deos immortales!
quae fuerit celeritas reditus eius, qui ingressus in
forum ardente curia, quae magnitudo animi, qui
vultus, quae oratio. Neque vero se populo solum,
sed etiam senatui commisit, neque senatui modo, sed
etiam publicis praesidiis et armis, neque his tantum,
verum etiam eius potestati, cui senatus totam rem
publicam, omnem Italiae pubem, cuncta populi Romani arma commiserat; cui numquam se hic profecto
tradidisset, nisi causae suae confideret, praesertim
omnia audienti, magna metuenti, multa suspicanti,
non nulla credenti. Magna vis est conscientiae,
iudices, et magna in utramque partem, ut neque
timeant, qui nihil commiserint, et poenam semper
62 ante oculos versari putent, qui peccarint. Neque
vero sine ratione certa causa Milonis semper a
senatu probata est. Videbant [enim] sapientissimi
homines facti rationem, praesentiam animi, defen-
presence of mind.

sionis constantiam. An vero obliti estis, iudices,
recenti illo nuntio necis Clodianae non modo inimicorum Milonis sermones et opiniones, sed non nullorum
etiam imperitorum? Negabant eum Romam esse
rediturum. Sive enim illud animo irato ac percito **63**
fecisset, ut incensus odio trucidaret inimicum, arbi-
trabantur eum tanti mortem P. Clodi putasse, ut
aequo animo patria careret, cum sanguine inimici
explesset odium suum; sive etiam illius morte
patriam liberare voluisset, non dubitaturum fortem
virum, quin, cum suo periculo salutem populo
Romano attulisset, cederet aequo animo legibus,
secum auferret gloriam sempiternam, vobis haec
fruenda relinqueret, quae ipse servasset. Multi
etiam Catilinam atque illa portenta loquebantur:
'Erumpet, occupabit aliquem locum, bellum patriae
faciet.' Miseros interdum cives optime de re publica
meritos, in quibus homines non modo res praeclarissi-
mas obliviscuntur, sed etiam nefarias suspicantur!
Ergo illa falsa fuerunt, quae certe vera extitissent, si **64**
Milo admisisset aliquid, quod non posset honeste
vereque defendere.

XXIV. Quid? quae postea sunt in eum congesta,
quae quemvis etiam mediocrium delictorum conscientia perculissent, ut sustinuit, di immortales!
Sustinuit! immo vero ut contempsit ac pro nihilo
putavit, quae neque maximo animo nocens neque
innocens nisi fortissimus vir neglegere potuisset!
Scutorum, gladiorum, frenorum pilorumque etiam
multitudo deprehendi posse indicabatur; nullum in
urbe vicum, nullum angiportum esse dicebant, in quo
non Miloni conducta esset domus; arma in villam

Ocriculanam devecta Tiberi, domus in clivo Capitolino scutis referta, plena omnia malleolorum ad urbis incendia comparatorum, haec non delata solum, sed paene credita, nec ante repudiata sunt quam quaesita. 65 Laudabam equidem incredibilem diligentiam Cn. Pompei, sed dicam, ut sentio, iudices. Nimis multa audire coguntur neque aliter facere possunt ii, quibus tota commissa est res publica. Quin etiam fuit audiendus popa Licinius nescio qui de circo maximo, servos Milonis apud se ebrios factos sibi confessos esse de interficiendo Pompeio coniurasse, dein postea se gladio percussum esse ab uno de illis, ne indicaret. Pompeio in hortos nuntiavit; arcessor in primis; de amicorum sententia rem defert ad senatum. Non poteram [in illius mei patriaeque custodis] tanta suspicione non metu exanimari, sed mirabar tamen credi popae, confessionem servorum audiri, vulnus in latere, quod acu punctum videretur, pro ictu gladia- 66 toris probari. Verum, ut intellego, cavebat magis Pompeius quam timebat non ea solum, quae timenda erant, sed omnia, ne vos aliquid timeretis. Oppugnata domus C. Caesaris, clarissimi et fortissimi viri, per multas noctis horas nuntiabatur. Nemo audierat tam celebri loco, nemo senserat; tamen audiebatur. Non poteram Cn. Pompeium, praestantissima virtute virum, timidum suspicari; diligentiam tota re publica suscepta nimiam nullam putabam. Frequentissimo senatu nuper in Capitolio senator inventus est, qui Milonem cum telo esse diceret. Nudavit se in sanctissimo templo, quoniam vita talis et civis et viri fidem non faciebat, ut eo tacente res ipsa loqueretur.

67   XXV. Omnia falsa atque insidiose ficta com-

perta sunt: cum tamen [si] metuitur etiam nunc
Milo, non iam hoc Clodianum crimen timemus, sed
tuas, Cn. Pompei, (te enim iam appello et ea voce, ut
me exaudire possis) [tuas,] tuas, inquam, suspiciones
perhorrescimus. Si Milonem times, si hunc de tua
vita nefarie aut nunc cogitare aut molitum aliquando
aliquid putas, si Italiae dilectus, ut non nulli conquisitores tui dictitarunt, si haec arma, si Capitolinae
cohortes, si excubiae, si vigiliae, si delecta iuventus,
quae tuum corpus domumque custodit, contra Milonis
impetum armata est atque illa omnia in hunc unum
instituta, parata, intenta sunt: magna in hoc certe
vis et incredibilis animus et non unius viri vires
atque opes iudicantur, siquidem in hunc unum et
praestantissimus dux electus et tota res publica
armata est. Sed quis non intellegit omnis tibi rei 68
publicae partis aegras et labantes, ut eas his armis
sanares et confirmares, esse commissas? Quodsi locus
Miloni datus esset, probasset profecto tibi ipsi
neminem umquam hominem homini cariorem fuisse
quam te sibi; nullum se umquam periculum pro tua
dignitate fugisse; cum illa ipsa taeterrima peste se
saepissime pro tua gloria contendisse; tribunatum
suum ad salutem meam, quae tibi carissima fuisset,
consiliis tuis gubernatum; se a te postea defensum in
periculo capitis, adiutum in petitione praeturae; duos
se habere semper amicissimos sperasse, te tuo beneficio, me suo. Quae si non probaret, si tibi ita
penitus inhaesisset ista suspicio, nullo ut evelli modo
posset, si denique Italia a dilectu, urbs ab armis sine
Milonis clade numquam esset conquietura, ne iste
haud dubitans cessisset patria, is qui ita natus est et

ita consuevit; te, Magne, tamen antestaretur, quod
69 nunc etiam facit.   XXVI. Vide, quam sit varia
vitae commutabilisque ratio, quam vaga volubilisque
fortuna, quantae infidelitates in amicitiis, quam ad
tempus aptae simulationes, quantae in periculis fugae
proximorum, quantae timiditates.   Erit, erit illud
profecto tempus, et illucescet aliquando ille dies, cum
tu salutaribus, ut spero, rebus tuis, sed fortasse
motu aliquo communium temporum (qui quam crebro
accidat, experti scire debemus), et amicissimi benevolentiam et gravissimi hominis fidem et unius post
homines natos fortissimi viri magnitudinem animi
70 desideres.   Quamquam quis hoc credat, Cn. Pompeium, iuris publici, moris maiorum, rei denique
publicae peritissimum, cum senatus ei commiserit,
ut videret, ne quid res publica detrimenti caperet,
quo uno versiculo satis armati semper consules
fuerunt etiam nullis armis datis, hunc exercitu, hunc
dilectu dato iudicium expectaturum fuisse in eius
consiliis vindicandis, qui vi iudicia ipsa tolleret?
Satis iudicatum est a Pompeio, satis, falso ista
conferri in Milonem, qui legem tulit, qua, ut ego
sentio, Milonem absolvi a vobis oporteret, ut omnes   *ASYNDETON*
71 confitentur, liceret.   Quod vero in illo loco atque   *(NO ET)*
illis publicorum praesidiorum copiis circumfusus
sedet, satis declarat se non terrorem inferre vobis
DIGNO + ABL.   (quid enim minus illo dignum quam cogere, ut vos
eum condemnetis, in quem animum advertere ipse et
more maiorum et suo iure posset?), sed praesidio
esse, ut intellegatis contra hesternam illam contionem
licere vobis, quod sentiatis, libere iudicare.
72   XXVII.   Nec vero me, iudices, Clodianum

crimen movet, nec tam sum demens tamque vestri
sensus ignarus atque expers, ut nesciam, quid de
morte Clodi sentiatis. De qua si iam nollem ita
diluere crimen, ut dilui, tamen inpune Miloni palam
clamare ac mentiri gloriose liceret: ' Occidi, occidi
non Sp. Maelium, qui annona levanda iacturisque rei
familiaris, quia nimis amplecti plebem videbatur,
in suspicionem incidit regni appetendi, non Ti.
Gracchum, qui collegae magistratum per seditionem
abrogavit, quorum interfectores inpleverunt orbem
terrarum nominis sui gloria, sed eum' (auderet enim
dicere, cum patriam periculo suo liberasset), 'cuius
nefandum adulterium in pulvinaribus sanctissimis
nobilissimae feminae conprehenderunt, eum, cuius 73
supplicio senatus sollemnes religiones expiandas
saepe censuit, eum, quem cum sorore germana
nefarium stuprum fecisse L. Lucullus iuratus se
quaestionibus habitis dixit comperisse, eum, qui
civem, quem senatus, quem populus Romanus, quem
omnes gentes urbis ac vitae civium conservatorem
iudicarant, servorum armis exterminavit, eum, qui
regna dedit, ademit, orbem terrarum, quibuscum
voluit, partitus est, eum, qui plurimis caedibus in
foro factis singulari virtute et gloria civem domum
vi et armis compulit, eum, cui nihil umquam nefas
fuit nec in facinore nec in libidine, eum, qui aedem
Nympharum incendit, ut memoriam publicam recen-
sionis tabulis publicis impressam extingueret, eum 74
denique, cui iam nulla lex erat, nullum civile ius,
nulli possessionum termini, qui non calumnia litium,
non iniustis vindiciis ac sacramentis alienos fundos,
sed castris, exercitu, signis inferendis petebat, qui

non solum Etruscos (eos enim penitus contempserat),
sed hunc P. Varium, fortissimum atque optimum
civem, iudicem nostrum, pellere possessionibus armis
castrisque conatus est, qui cum architectis et decem-
pedis villas multorum hortosque peragrabat, qui
Ianiculo et Alpibus spem possessionum terminarat
suarum, qui cum ab equite Romano splendido et
forti, M. Paconio, non impetrasset, ut sibi insulam in
lacu Prilio venderet, repente lintribus in eam insulam
materiem, calcem, caementa, arma convexit dominoque
trans ripam inspectante non dubitavit extruere aedi-
75 ficium in alieno, qui huic T. Furfanio, cui viro, di
immortales! (quid enim ego de muliercula Scantia,
quid de adulescente P. Apinio dicam? quorum utrique mortem est minitatus, nisi sibi hortorum possessione cessissent) — sed ausum esse T. Furfanio dicere,
si sibi pecuniam, quantam poposcerat, non dedisset,
mortuum se in domum eius inlaturum, qua invidia
huic esset tali viro conflagrandum; qui Appium
fratrem, hominem mihi coniunctum fidissima gratia,
absentem de possessione fundi deiecit, qui parietem
sic per vestibulum sororis instituit ducere, sic agere
fundamenta, ut sororem non modo vestibulo privaret,
sed omni aditu et limine.'

76   XXVIII.   Quamquam haec quidem iam tolerabilia videbantur, etsi aequaliter in rem publicam,
in privatos, in longinquos, in propinquos, in alienos,
in suos irruebat; sed nescio quo modo iam usu obdu-
ruerat et percalluerat civitatis incredibilis patientia.
Quae vero aderant iam et impendebant, quonam
modo ea aut depellere potuissetis aut ferre? Imperium ille si nactus esset — omitto socios, exteras

nationes, reges, tetrarchas; vota enim faceretis, ut
in eos se potius inmitteret quam in vestras posses-
siones, vestra tecta, vestras pecunias — pecunias
dico; a liberis [medius fidius] et a coniugibus vestris
numquam ille effrenatas suas libidines cohibuisset.
Fingi haec putatis, quae patent, quae nota sunt
omnibus, quae tenentur, servorum exercitus illum in
urbe conscripturum fuisse, per quos totam rem
publicam resque privatas omnium possideret? Quam **77**
ob rem, si cruentum gladium tenens clamaret T.
Annius: 'Adeste, quaeso, atque audite, cives! P.
Clodium interfeci, eius furores, quos nullis iam
legibus, nullis iudiciis frenare poteramus, hoc ferro
et hac dextera a cervicibus vestris reppuli, per me
ut unum ius, aequitas, leges, libertas, pudor, pudicitia
in civitate maneret': esset vero timendum, quonam
modo id ferret civitas. Nunc enim quis est, qui non
probet, qui non laudet, qui non unum post hominum
memoriam T. Annium plurimum rei publicae profuisse,
maxima laetitia populum Romanum, cunctam Italiam,
nationes omnes affecisse et dicat et sentiat? Non queo,
vetera illa populi Romani gaudia quanta fuerint, iudicare; multas tamen iam summorum imperatorum
clarissimas victorias aetas nostra vidit, quarum nulla
neque tam diuturnam attulit laetitiam nec tantam.
Mandate hoc memoriae, iudices. Spero multa vos **78**
liberosque vestros in re publica bona esse visuros; in
iis singulis ita semper existimabitis, vivo P. Clodio
nihil eorum vos visuros fuisse. In spem maximam et,
quem ad modum confido, verissimam sumus adducti
hunc ipsum annum hoc ipso summo viro consule com-
pressa hominum licentia, cupiditatibus fractis, legibus

et iudiciis constitutis salutarem civitati fore.   Num
quis est igitur tam demens, qui hoc P. Clodio vivo
contingere potuisse arbitretur?   Quid? ea, quae
tenetis privata atque vestra, dominante homine
furioso quod ius perpetuae possessionis habere potuissent?

XXIX.   Non timeo, iudices, ne odio inimicitiarum mearum inflammatus lubentius haec in illum
evomere videar quam verius.   Etenim, si praecipuum
esse debebat, tamen ita communis erat omnium ille
hostis, ut in communi odio paene aequaliter versa-
retur odium meum.   Non potest dici satis, ne cogitari
quidem, quantum in illo sceleris, quantum exitii
79 fuerit.   Quin sic attendite, iudices.   Nempe haec
est quaestio de interitu P. Clodi.   Fingite animis
(liberae sunt enim nostrae cogitationes et, quae
volunt, sic intuentur, ut ea cernimus, quae videmus),
fingite igitur cogitatione imaginem huius condicionis
meae, si possim efficere, ut Milonem absolvatis, sed
ita, si P. Clodius revixerit.   Quid vultu extimuistis?
quonam modo ille vos vivus afficeret, quos mortuus
inani cogitatione percussit?   Quid? si ipse Cn. Pompeius, qui ea virtute ac fortuna est, ut ea potuerit
semper quae nemo praeter illum, si is, inquam,
potuisset aut quaestionem de morte P. Clodi ferre aut
ipsum ab inferis excitare, utrum putatis potius
facturum fuisse?   Etiamsi propter amicitiam vellet
illum ab inferis avocare, propter rem publicam non
fecisset.   Eius igitur mortis sedetis ultores, cuius
vitam si putetis per vos restitui posse, nolitis, et de
eius nece lata quaestio est, qui si lege eadem revivis-
cere posset, lata lex numquam esset.   Huius ergo

interfector si esset, in confitendo ab iisne poenam
timeret, quos liberavisset? Graeci homines deorum 80
honores tribuunt iis viris, qui tyrannos necaverunt.
(Quae ego vidi Athenis, quae aliis in urbibus Grae-
ciae! quas res divinas talibus institutas viris, quos
cantus, quae carmina! Prope ad immortalitatis et
religionem et memoriam consecrantur); vos tanti
conservatorem populi, tanti sceleris ultorem non
modo honoribus nullis afficietis, sed etiam ad sup-
plicium rapi patiemini? Confiteretur, inquam, si
fecisset, et magno animo et libenter fecisse se libertatis omnium causa, quod esset ei non confitendum
modo, verum etiam praedicandum. XXX. Etenim, 81
si id non negat, ex quo nihil petit, nisi ut ignoscatur,
dubitaret id fateri, ex quo etiam praemia laudis essent
petenda? nisi vero gratius putat esse vobis sui se
capitis quam vestri defensorem fuisse; cum praesertim
in ea confessione, si grati esse velletis, honores
assequeretur amplissimos. Si factum vobis non
probaretur (quamquam qui poterat salus sua cuiquam
non probari?), sed tamen si minus fortissimi viri
virtus civibus grata cecidisset, magno animo con-
stantique cederet ex ingrata civitate. Nam quid
esset ingratius quam laetari ceteros, lugere eum
solum, propter quem ceteri laetarentur? Quamquam 82
hoc animo semper omnes fuimus in patriae proditori-
bus opprimendis, ut, quoniam nostra futura esset
gloria, periculum quoque et invidiam nostram putare-
mus. Nam quae mihi ipsi tribuenda laus esset, cum
tantum in consulatu meo pro vobis ac liberis vestris
ausus essem, si id, quod conabar, sine maximis
dimicationibus meis me esse ausurum arbitrarer?

Quae mulier sceleratum ac perniciosum civem interficere non auderet, si periculum non timeret? Proposita invidia, morte, poena qui nihilo segnius rem
publicam defendit, is vir vere putandus est. Populi
grati est praemiis afficere bene meritos de re publica
civis, viri fortis ne suppliciis quidem moveri, ut
83 fortiter fecisse paeniteat. Quam ob rem uteretur
eadem confessione T. Annius qua Ahala, qua Nasica,
qua Opimius, qua Marius, qua nosmet ipsi; et, si grata
res publica esset, laetaretur; si ingrata, tamen in
gravi fortuna conscientia sua niteretur.

Sed huius beneficii gratiam, iudices, fortuna
populi Romani et vestra felicitas et di immortales
sibi deberi putant. Nec vero quisquam aliter arbi-
trari potest, nisi qui nullam vim esse ducit numenve
divinum, quem neque imperii nostri magnitudo neque
sol ille nec caeli signorumque motus nec vicissitudines
rerum atque ordines movent neque, id quod maximum est, maiorum sapientia, qui sacra, qui caeri-
monias, qui auspicia et ipsi sanctissime coluerunt
84 et nobis suis posteris prodiderunt. XXXI. Est, est
profecto illa vis, neque in his corporibus atque in hac
inbecillitate nostra inest quiddam, quod vigeat et
sentiat, non inest in hoc tanto naturae tam praeclaro
motu. Nisi forte idcirco non putant, quia non
apparet nec cernitur; proinde quasi nostram ipsam
mentem, qua sapimus, qua providemus, qua haec
ipsa agimus ac dicimus, videre aut plane, qualis aut
ubi sit, sentire possimus. Ea vis igitur ipsa, quae
saepe incredibiles huic urbi felicitates atque opes
attulit, illam perniciem extinxit ac sustulit, cui
primum mentem iniecit, ut vi irritare ferroque laces-

sere fortissimum virum auderet vincereturque ab eo,
quem si vicisset, habiturus esset impunitatem et
licentiam sempiternam. Non est humano consilio, 85
ne mediocri quidem, iudices, deorum immortalium
cura res illa perfecta. Religiones mehercule ipsae,
quae illam beluam cadere viderunt, commosse se
videntur et ius in illo suum retinuisse. Vos enim
iam, Albani tumuli atque luci, vos, inquam, imploro
atque obtestor, vosque, Albanorum obrutae arae
sacrorum populi Romani sociae et aequales, quas
ille praeceps amentia caesis prostratisque sanctissimis
lucis substructionum insanis molibus oppresserat;
vestrae tum irae, vestrae religiones viguerunt, vestra
vis valuit, quam ille omni scelere polluerat; tuque ex
tuo edito monte, Latiaris sancte Iuppiter, cuius ille
lacus, nemora finesque saepe omni nefario stupro et
scelere macularat, aliquando ad eum puniendum
oculos aperuisti; vobis illae, vobis vestro in conspectu
serae, sed iustae tamen et debitae poenae solutae
sunt. Nisi forte hoc etiam casu factum esse dicemus, 86
ut ante ipsum sacrarium Bonae deae, quod est in
fundo T. Sergi Galli, in primis honesti et ornati
adulescentis, ante ipsam, inquam, Bonam deam, cum
proelium commisisset, primum illud volnus acciperet,
quo taeterrimam mortem obiret, ut non absolutus
iudicio illo nefario videretur, sed ad hanc insignem
poenam reservatus. XXXII. Nec vero non eadem
ira deorum hanc eius satellitibus iniecit amentiam, ut
sine imaginibus, sine cantu atque ludis, sine exequiis,
sine lamentis, sine laudationibus, sine funere, oblitus
cruore et luto, spoliatus illius supremi diei celebritate, cui cedere inimici etiam solent, ambureretur

abiectus. Non fuisse credo fas clarissimorum virorum formas illi taeterrimo parricidae aliquid decoris afferre, neque ullo in loco potius mortem eius lacerari, quam in quo esset vita damnata.

87　　Dura medius fidius mihi iam Fortuna populi Romani et crudelis videbatur, quae tot annos illum in hanc rem publicam insultare pateretur. Polluerat stupro sanctissimas religiones, senatus gravissima decreta perfregerat, pecunia se a iudicibus palam redemerat, vexarat in tribunatu senatum, omnium ordinum consensu pro salute rei publicae gesta resciderat, me patria expulerat, bona diripuerat, domum incenderat, liberos, coniugem meam vexarat, Cn. Pompeio nefarium bellum indixerat, magistratuum privatorumque caedes effecerat, domum mei fratris incenderat, vastarat Etruriam, multos sedibus ac fortunis eiecerat; instabat, urgebat; capere eius amentiam civitas, Italia, provinciae, regna non poterant; incidebantur iam domi leges, quae nos servis nostris addicerent; nihil erat cuiusquam, quod quidem ille adamasset, quod non hoc anno suum fore

88 putaret. Obstabat eius cogitationibus nemo praeter Milonem. Illum ipsum, qui obstare poterat, novo reditu in gratiam quasi devinctum arbitrabatur; Caesaris potentiam suam esse dicebat; bonorum animos in meo casu contempserat; Milo unus urgebat.

　　XXXIII. Hic di immortales, ut supra dixi, mentem illi perdito ac furioso dederunt, ut huic faceret insidias. Aliter perire pestis illa non potuit; numquam illum res publica suo iure esset ulta. Senatus, credo, praetorem eum circumscripsisset. Ne cum solebat quidem id facere, in privato eodem hoc aliquid profecerat. An consules in praetore coër- **89** cendo fortes fuissent? Primum Milone occiso habuisset suos consules; deinde quis in eo praetore consul fortis esset, per quem tribunum virtutem consularem crudelissime vexatam esse meminisset? Oppressisset omnia, possideret, teneret; lege nova, quae est inventa apud eum cum reliquis legibus Clodianis, servos nostros libertos suos fecisset; postremo, nisi eum di immortales in eam mentem inpulissent, ut homo effeminatus fortissimum virum conaretur occidere, hodie rem publicam nullam haberetis. An ille praetor, ille vero consul, si modo haec **90** templa atque ipsa moenia stare eo vivo tamdiu et consulatum eius expectare potuissent, ille denique vivus mali nihil fecisset, qui mortuus uno ex suis satellitibus [Sex. Clodio] duce curiam incenderit? Quo quid miserius, quid acerbius, quid luctuosius vidimus, templum sanctitatis, amplitudinis, mentis, consilii publici, caput urbis, aram sociorum, portum omnium gentium, sedem ab universo populo concessam uni ordini inflammari, excindi, funestari, neque id fieri a multitudine imperita, quamquam esset miserum id ipsum, sed ab uno? Qui cum tantum ausus sit ustor pro mortuo, quid signifer pro vivo non esset ausus? In curiam potissimum abiecit, ut eam mortuus incenderet, quam vivus everterat. Et sunt, qui de via Appia querantur, taceant de **91** curia, et qui ab eo spirante forum putent potuisse defendi, cuius non restiterit cadaveri curia? Excitate, excitate ipsum, si potestis, a mortuis; frangetis impetum vivi, cuius vix sustinetis furias insepulti?

Nisi vero sustinuistis eos, qui cum facibus ad curiam cucurrerunt, cum falcibus ad Castoris, cum gladiis toto foro volitarunt. Caedi vidistis populum Romanum, contionem gladiis disturbari, cum audiretur silentio M. Caelius, tribunus pl., vir et in re publica fortissimus et in suscepta causa firmissimus et bonorum voluntati et auctoritati senatus deditus et in hac Milonis sive invidia sive fortuna singulari divina et incredibili fide.

92   XXXIV. Sed iam satis multa de causa, extra causam etiam nimis fortasse multa. Quid restat, nisi ut orem obtesterque vos, iudices, ut eam misericordiam tribuatis fortissimo viro, quam ipse non implorat, ego etiam repugnante hoc et imploro et exposco? Nolite, si in nostro omnium fletu nullam lacrimam aspexistis Milonis, si vultum semper eundem, si vocem, si orationem stabilem ac non mutatam videtis, hoc minus ei parcere; haud scio an multo sit etiam adiuvandus magis. Etenim, si in gladiatoriis pugnis et *in* infimi generis hominum condicione atque fortuna timidos atque supplices et, ut vivere liceat, obsecrantis etiam odisse solemus, fortis atque animosos et se acriter ipsos morti offerentes servare cupimus, eorumque nos magis miseret, qui nostram misericordiam non requirunt, quam qui illam efflagitant, quanto hoc

93 magis in fortissimis civibus facere debemus! Me quidem, iudices, exanimant et interimunt hae voces Milonis, quas audio assidue et quibus intersum cottidie. 'Valeant,' inquit, 'valeant cives mei; sint incolumes, sint florentes, sint beati; stet haec urbs praeclara mihique patria carissima, quoquo modo erit merita de me; tranquilla re publica mei cives, quoniam mihi

cum illis non licet, sine me ipsi, sed propter me tamen perfruantur. Ego cedam atque abibo. Si mihi bona re publica frui non licuerit, at carebo mala et, quam primum tetigero bene moratam et liberam civitatem, in ea conquiescam. O frustra,' inquit, 94 'mihi suscepti labores, o spes fallaces et cogitationes inanes meae! Ego cum tribunus pl. re publica oppressa me senatui dedissem, quem extinctum acceperam, equitibus Romanis, quorum vires erant debiles, bonis viris, qui omnem auctoritatem Clodianis armis abiecerant, mihi umquam bonorum praesidium defuturum putarem? Ego cum te' (mecum enim saepissime loquitur) 'patriae reddidissem, mihi putarem in patria non futurum locum? Ubi nunc senatus est, quem secuti sumus, ubi equites Romani illi, illi,' inquit, 'tui, ubi studia municipiorum, ubi Italiae voces, ubi denique tua illa, M. Tulli, quae plurimis fuit auxilio, vox atque defensio? Mihine ea soli, qui pro te totiens morti me obtuli, nihil potest opitulari?'

XXXV. Nec vero haec, iudices, ut ego nunc 95 flens, sed hoc eodem loquitur vultu, quo videtis. Negat enim se, negat ingratis civibus fecisse, quae fecerit, timidis et omnia circumspicientibus pericula non negat. Plebem et infimam multitudinem, quae P. Clodio duce fortunis vestris imminebat, eam, quo tutior esset vestra vita, se fecisse commemorat ut non modo virtute flecteret, sed etiam tribus suis patrimoniis deleniret, nec timet, ne, cum plebem muneribus placarit, vos non conciliarit meritis in rem publicam singularibus. Senatus erga se benevolentiam temporibus his ipsis saepe esse perspectam, vestras vero et vestrorum ordinum occursationes, studia, sermones, quemcumque cursum fortuna dederit, *se* secum abla-

96 turum esse dicit.   Meminit etiam sibi vocem praeconis modo defuisse, quam minime desiderarit, populi vero cunctis suffragiis, quod unum cupierit, se consulem declaratum; nunc denique, si haec contra se sint futura, sibi facinoris suspicionem, non facti crimen obstare.   Addit haec, quae certe vera sunt, fortis et sapientis viros non tam praemia sequi solere recte factorum quam ipsa recte facta; se nihil in vita nisi praeclarissime fecisse, siquidem nihil sit praestabilius viro quam periculis patriam liberare;   Beatos esse, quibus ea res honori fuerit a suis civibus, nec tamen

97 eos miseros, qui beneficio cives suos vicerint.   Sed tamen ex omnibus praemiis virtutis, si esset habenda ratio praemiorum, amplissimum esse praemium gloriam; esse hanc unam, quae brevitatem vitae posteritatis memoria consolaretur, quae efficeret, ut absentes adessemus, mortui viveremus.   Hanc denique esse, cuius gradibus etiam in caelum homines viderentur

98 ascendere.   'De me,' inquit, 'semper populus Romanus, semper omnes gentes loquentur, nulla umquam obmutescet vetustas.   Quin hoc tempore ipso, cum omnes a meis inimicis faces invidiae meae subiciantur, tamen omni in hominum coetu gratiis agendis et gratulationibus habendis et omni sermone celebramur.   Omitto Etruriae festos et actos et institutos dies.   Centesima lux est haec ab interitu P. Clodi et, opinor, altera.   Qua fines imperii populi Romani sunt, ea non solum fama iam de illo, sed etiam laetitia peragravit.   Quam ob rem, ubi corpus hoc sit, non,' inquit, 'laboro, quoniam omnibus in terris

et iam versatur et semper habitabit nominis mei gloria.'

XXXVI.   Haec tu mecum saepe his absentibus ; 99 sed isdem audientibus haec ego tecum, Milo : 'Te quidem, cum isto animo es, satis laudare non possum, sed, quo est ista magis divina virtus, eo maiore a te dolore divellor.   Nec vero, si mihi eriperis, reliqua est illa tamen ad consolandum querella, ut iis irasci possim, a quibus tantum vulnus accepero.   Non enim inimici mei te mihi eripient, sed amicissimi, non male aliquando de me meriti, sed semper optime.' Nullum umquam, iudices, mihi tantum dolorem inuretis (etsi quis potest esse tantus ?), sed ne hunc quidem ipsum, ut obliviscar, quanti me semper fece- ritis.   Quae si vos cepit oblivio, aut si in me aliquid offendistis, cur non id meo capite potius luitur quam Milonis ?   Praeclare enim vixero, si quid mihi ac- ciderit, priusquam hoc tantum mali videro.   Nunc 100 me una consolatio sustentat, quod tibi, T. Anni, nullum a me amoris, nullum studii, nullum pietatis officium defuit.   Ego inimicitias potentium pro te appetivi, ego meum saepe corpus et vitam obieci armis inimicorum tuorum, ego me plurimis pro te supplicem abieci, bona, fortunas meas ac liberorum meorum in communionem tuorum temporum contuli ; hoc denique ipso die si quae vis est parata, si quae dimicatio capitis futura, deposco.   Quid iam restat ? quid habeo, quod faciam pro tuis in me meritis, nisi ut eam fortunam, quaecumque erit tua, ducam meam? Non recuso, non abnuo, vosque obsecro, iudices, ut vestra beneficia, quae in me contulistis, aut in huius salute augeatis aut in eiusdem exitio occasura esse videatis.

101   XXXVII.   His lacrimis non movetur Milo; est quodam incredibili robore animi; exilium ibi esse putat, ubi virtuti non sit locus; mortem naturae finem esse, non poenam.   Sed hic ea mente, qua natus est; quid? vos, iudices, quo tandem animo eritis?   Memoriam Milonis retinebitis, ipsum eicietis? Et erit dignior locus in terris ullus, qui hanc virtutem excipiat, quam hic, qui procreavit?   Vos, vos appello, fortissimi viri, qui multum pro re publica sanguinem effudistis; vos in viri et in civis invicti periculo appello, centuriones, vosque, milites; vobis non modo inspectantibus, sed etiam armatis et huic iudicio praesidentibus haec tanta virtus ex hac urbe expelle-

102 tur, exterminabitur, proicietur?   O me miserum, o me infelicem!   Revocare tu me in patriam, Milo, potuisti per hos, ego te in patria per eosdem retinere non potero?   Quid respondebo liberis meis, qui te parentem alterum putant? quid tibi, Quinte frater, qui nunc abes, consorti mecum temporum illorum? mene non potuisse Milonis salutem tueri per eosdem, per quos nostram ille servasset?   At in qua causa non potuisse?   Quae est grata gentibus *** non potuisse?   Iis, qui maxime P. Clodi morte adquierunt.

103 Quo deprecante?   Me.   Quodnam ego concepi tantum scelus aut quod in me tantum facinus admisi, iudices, cum illa indicia communis exitii indagavi, patefeci, protuli, extinxi?   Omnes in me meosque redundant ex fonte illo dolores.   Quid me reducem esse voluistis? an ut inspectante me expellerentur hi, per quos essem restitutus?   Nolite, obsecro vos, acerbiorem mihi pati reditum esse, quam fuerit ille ipse discessus.   Nam qui possum putare me restitutum esse, si distrahar ab his, per quos restitutus sum?

XXXVIII. Utinam di immortales fecissent (pace tua, patria, dixerim ; metuo enim, ne scelerate dicam in te, quod pro Milone dicam pie), utinam P. Clodius non modo viveret, sed etiam praetor, consul, dictator esset potius, quam hoc spectaculum viderem ! O, di **104** immortales, fortem et a vobis, iudices, conservandum virum ! 'Minime, minime,' inquit. 'Immo vero poenas ille debitas luerit ; nos subeamus, si ita necesse est, non debitas.' Hicine vir patriae natus usquam nisi in patria morietur aut, si forte, pro patria ? huius vos animi monumenta retinebitis, corporis in Italia nullum sepulcrum esse patiemini ? hunc sua quisquam sententia ex hac urbe expellet, quem omnes urbes expulsum a vobis ad se vocabunt ? O terram illam beatam, quae hunc virum exceperit, **105** hanc ingratam, si eiecerit, miseram, si amiserit ! Sed finis sit ; neque enim prae lacrimis iam loqui possum, et hic se lacrimis defendi vetat. Vos oro obtestorque, iudices, ut in sententiis ferendis, quod sentietis, id audeatis. Vestram virtutem, iustitiam, fidem, mihi credite, is maxime probabit, qui in iudicibus legendis optimum et sapientissimum et fortissimum quemque elegit.

NOTES.

ABBREVIATIONS

L. and S. = Lewis and Short's Lat. Dict.	Näg. = Nägelsbach, Stilistik.
R. = Roby's Lat. Grammar.	C. = Cicero.
Madv. = Madvig's Lat. Grammar.	Cl. = Clodius.
Zumpt = Zumpt's Lat. Grammar.	M. = Milo.
K. = Kennedy's Lat. Grammar.	
Clark = A. C. Clark, Anecdota Oxoniensia (Classical), part VII.	

C. I. § 1. novi iudicii. The procedure as well as the constitution of the court was in many respects new; v. Introd., page xiv.

nova forma explained below. The absence of the usual audience and the presence of the soldiers.

requirunt, 'look in vain for.'

consuetudinem fori, &c., 'the customary sights of the forum and the established practice of the law courts.'

non enim corona. A Roman trial was generally attended by a number of interested auditors, called the 'corona' or ring. To these the orator's words were often as much addressed as to the jury. Cf. e.g. the beginning of the Archias, and Pro Flacco § 69 *oratio a iudicibus avertitur: vox in coronam turbamque effunditur.* The *corona* was distinct from the *turba* (here *frequentia*) of the general public who often thronged the forum. On this occasion the *corona* was absent. There *was a frequentia* but *non usitata.* Lucan perhaps alludes to this passage in Phars. I. 319 :

> ' quis castra timenti
> nescit mixta foro, gladii quum triste minantes
> iudicium insolita trepidum cinxere corona?'

where the court is surrounded by a *corona* in the military instead of the forensic sense.

§ 2. pro templis. The soldiers prevented the temples being occupied as they often were by rioters.

contra vim, 'to protect us against violence.'

non...non afferunt tamen oratori aliquid, cannot fail to produce an effect (upon the speaker). *Oratori* is better omitted.

in foro et in iudicio, i.e. where one would least expect intimidation.

tamen ne non timere quidem, &c., ' our very freedom from fear necessarily involves some fear.'

tempori, a noticeable word of Cicero's meaning often crisis, emergency, almost danger. Thus the title of Cicero's poem *de temporibus meis* = ' my adventures,' i.e. the time of his banishment and restoration.

consilium, ' good sense ' made up of *sapientia* and *justitia*.

qui nec putaret—would *never* have thought it compatible, &c. Cp. Hor. Odes, IV. 6. 12 &c. *ille non inclusus...falleret :* he *was not the man* to deceive his foes. The suppressed protasis is ' if placed in circumstances where other men might act otherwise.'

tradere...dedere, *dedere* a word peculiarly used of *surrender to an enemy, tradere* is applied to any act of consigning or committing.

temeritas, ' reckless passion.'

concitatae, ' lashed into excitement,' often found with words like *concio, populus* and *multitudo.*

auctoritate publica, ' state support,' i.e. the encouragement which would be given to the mob by feeling that they had the government at their back.

§ 3. non periculum sed praesidium denuntiant, almost a zeugma, for *denuntiare aliquid alicui* elsewhere in Cicero = ' threaten,' cp. Philippic XIV. 8 *omnibus pestem vastitatem cruciatum tormenta denuntiant.*

silentium, a cut at Pompey! for the troops as a matter of fact had not maintained silence.

quae quidem, that part *at least* which does consist of citizens. Cp. Brutus 17 *Catonem vero quis nostrorum oratorum, qui quidem nunc sunt, legit ?* R. § 1693. C. means that the Clodians were all slaves and foreigners, at any rate not properly qualified citizens. This is of course not really true.

C. II. eorum, gen. of definition—' namely those.'

omnibus exitiis publicis, ' everything that can possibly destroy the state.'

hesterna etiam contione, ' as late as yesterday's meeting'— temporal use of *etiam,* found generally with some other temporal phrase or adverb as *tum, nunc, vixdum, quamdiu.* Cp. *quamdiu* *etiam* Cat. **I. 1. It** is sometimes found with verbs, which describe a merely temporary state, thus *etiam cubans*—'still in bed,' *etiam spirans*—'still alive.'

pavit, 'has glutted,' a contemptuous word. Cp. Clu. 72 *ille improbissimus quaestu iudicario pastus.*

praeire, quid iudicaretis, 'dictate what verdict you should give.' *Praeire voce* or *verbis* is to recite a formula (as in our Marriage Service) for someone else to repeat. This was regularly done when an oath was taken or a building consecrated. But perhaps Cicero may be thinking of a school lesson. Cp. Quint. I. 2, 12 *lectio non omnis praeeunte eget,* and the common use of *dictata* = lessons.

quid iudicaretis, here as in *lugeamus* § 4 the subjunctive does double duty. The direct question would be dubitative and therefore in the subjunctive: each juryman would ask himself *quid iudicem?* v. Näg. § 98, R. § 1612.

ut eum civem retineatis, 'retain *as* citizen him' &c. Cf. Philippic VIII. 16 *ego Clodium perniciosum civem arbitrabar, tu retinendum civem.*

§ 4. adeste animis, 'be present with your minds,' i.e. 'collect yourselves'; a common exhortation to (1) courage, (2) attention, according to circumstances, here the former.

amplissimorum ordinum. The Judices were at this time selected from the Senate, Knights and Tribuni Aerarii. These last are sometimes spoken of as a separate 'ordo.' At other times they seem to be classed with the knights. Thus by *amplissimi ordines* C. may simply mean the senators and knights. What exactly the *tribuni aerarii* were is an obscure question. For a clear account of what is known of them, the student may be referred to Heitland Pro Rabirio, App. G.

quae vultu, observe the antithesis—*vultu* (looks) with *re* (actions), *verbis* (ordinary words) with *sententiis* (formal verdicts), *significo* (hint) with *declaro* (openly express). Cp. Ad Fam. I. 9. 17 *idque non solum fronte ac vultu, quibus simulatio facile sustinetur declarant, sed etiam sententia* (MSS. *sensu*) *saepe iam tabellaque docuerunt.*

auctoritati, i.e. the authority of the law courts, which Clodius' actions tended to subvert (compare *vi iudicia tolleret* § 70). But perhaps (as certainly in other places e.g. § 34) the Judices are addressed as the representatives of the 'boni' or well-affected citizens in general.

dediti, 'devoted supporters of.' Cp. *auctoritati senatus deditus,* § 91.

lugeamus, v. on *iudicaretis,* § 3.

§ 5. exercitum, 'sorely tried.' Cp. Att. i. 11, 2 *scito nihil tam exercitum esse nunc Romae quam candidatos* (where we also find the neuter for masc.). ' Quis miserior ' and ' quid miserius ' differ in strength as 'a miserable object,' from 'a miserable person.' Cf. Phil. ii. 33 *quid beatius illis, &c.*

amplissimorum praemiorum, the state offices, which citizens who entered public life (*res publica*) hoped to win.

equidem ceteras, &c. *equidem* is answered by *vero* in next sentence: *dumtaxat* 'at least.' So Edd. But perhaps it is more correct to say that *dumtaxat*='but only,' and itself answers *equidem*. v. Reid on *dumtaxat* in De Amic. § 53 where he derives *taxat* from the root of *tangere=denken=*think.

sentire pro bonis, the usual phrase is *sentire bene* or *sentire cum bonis.* *Sentio* is regularly used of political views.

ex cunctis ordinibus, above the *Judices* were *ex amplissimis ordinibus,* here they are *ex cunctis.* The explanation, I believe, is that *ordo* may signify a classification either by social status or by occupation. In the first sense, the senators and the knights are *ordines*; so too we have *ordo libertinorum.* In the second sense we have *ordo scribarum aratorum, &c.* In the first sense the *Judices* came from the 2 (or 3) *amplissimi ordines.* In the second sense they came or might come from all professions v. Heitland on Pro Rab. § 27, who however takes *ordo* there to mean a ' company.' (Cp. also Wilkins on Pro Lege Man. § 18.)

iudicarent, subj. because *in eo in quo=in tali ut.*

numquam existimavi. ' I never thought that Milo's enemies would have any hope of employing such men as these even to lower his position, far less to accomplish his destruction.' Not only did *salutem extinguere* seem impossible, but even the far easier *gloriam infringere.*

non modo=*non dicam.* Cp. the very similar antithesis in Planc. § 78 *putas...ullam esse tantam contentionem quam ego non modo pro salute tua sed etiam pro dignitate defugerim.*

spem habere ad. Halm quotes Att. xv. 20. 2 *spem habere ad vivendum.* ' The accusative of the gerund with *ad* often alternates with the genitive,' Roby § 1313, who quotes *conatus ad erumpendum, mora ad dimicandum,* etc.

§ 6. quamquam, connexive, ' and yet.'

abuti, not quite so strong as our ' abuse,' rather ' strain to the utmost,' ' take advantage of.' Cp. Pro Sulla § 47, *noli lenitate mea abuti* (and Reid's note).

nisi oculis videritis. It seems to me a confusion to quote the rhetorical figure ἐνάργεια or ὑποτύπωσις, which is simply a technical term for ' graphic description ' (v. Sandys on Orator,

139). Several passages in this speech do no doubt supply examples of this figure, but C. cannot mean 'don't acquit M. unless I give you a graphic description.' Rather 'unless I give you evidence as convincing as that of your own eyes.' So *hac luce clariores* below. A more accurate expression is *videri cernere oculis*, Rosc. Am. 98, Clu. 66.

insidias facere alicui, 'to make a treacherous attack upon.'

salus vestra, the more usual construction is *saluti vobis.* The nominative is more rhetorical and forcible : so we sometimes find *exitium* for *exitio,* e.g. Verr. Act. I. 12 *cuius legatio fuit exitium totius Asiae.*

clariores hac luce, 'clear as daylight.'

C. III. § 7. ad eam orationem, 'to that part of my speech': as 'oratio' properly = 'speaking,' it is naturally as applicable to a part as the whole of a speech, cp. Rosc. Am. 129 *in extrema oratione nostra,* De Or. II. 114 *omnis illa oratio, quae sit propria quaestionis et iudicii.*

rem plane, quae veniat. According to Edd. indirect question with subject drawn into the principal sentence, cp. Pro Deiot. § 30 *quis tuum patrem, quis esset, audivit,* Madv. § 439. But the cases quoted there are hardly analogous to this, and the subjunctive may be sufficiently explained as dependent on another subjunctive, Roby § 1778.

tandem, 'pray,' **nempe,** 'why.' The two words add a tone of astonishment to question and answer respectively.

quae...vidit &c. Translate carefully. 'Which witnessed as its first capital trial that of M. Horatius.' The trial of Horatius is so called because, according to the tradition, it was the first instance of *provocatio* or appeal to the people assembled in the comitia centuriata and thus the first *iudicium populi.*

nondum libera civitate, 'even in the days of despotism.'

§ 8. recte, 'morally right,' *recte* is to *iure,* as *fas* is to *ius.*

nisi vero : this phrase (and also *nisi forte*) are often used to introduce an alternative which is obviously untenable and therefore proves the previous statement by a *reductio ad absurdum. Nisi vero* is always used in this ironical sense, *nisi forte* not always (Madv. § 442 c, Obs. 1).

iure caesum videri. Velleius Paterculus 2, 414 gives the answer of Africanus thus *si is occupandae rei publicae animum habuisset, iure caesum videri.* Cic. De Or. II. 106 and Valerius Maximus 6, 2, 3 give it as here.

Ahala ille Servilius. Observe the *cognomen* put before the *nomen* : v. Tyrrell on Ep. CCI. who says that Cicero almost always uses this order, both in his speeches and letters, if the *praenomen* is omitted.   The cases of Ahala and Nasica are appealed to by Cicero in much the same way, Cat. I. 1.

ille, 'in old days,' contrasting Ahala (in the 5th century) with the more modern examples that follow, cp. Pro Sull. § 23 *nemo istuc Marco illi Catoni seni...nemo huic nostro C. Mario obiecit,* Pro Man. § 22 *Medea illa quondam profugisse dicitur.*

aut me consule senatus.   Cicero has no reason for thus separating his case from those of Marius and Opimius, who both, like him, acted under a *senatus consultum ultimum* (v. on § 70).   Nasica on the other hand was a *privatus* and had no such authority, v. Cat. I. § 3.

doctissimi, a not unfrequent epithet of poets, cp. Hor. Od. I. 1, 29, *doctarum frontium,* where Wickham traces the epithet to the σοφὸς ἀοιδὸς of heroic times.   It is perhaps rather applied to Roman poets as *learned* in Greek legendary lore (so often to Catullus).   The *doctissimi* here are perhaps not only Aeschylus, through whose Eumenides *we* know the story of Orestes, but also Latin tragedians, such as Ennius, Pacuvius &c., cp. Rosc. Am. 66 and 67, and Verg. Aen. IV. 471 *aut Agamemnonius scenis agitatus Orestes.*

eum, i.e. Orestes, v. Classical dictionary.

variatis hominum sententiis, 'when human opinion was divided.'

§ 9.   **duodecim tabulae,** cp. Pro Tullio § 47.   The words of the law were *si nox furtum factum sit, si im occisit, iure caesus esto, luci, si se telo defendit* (*nox = noctu*).

quoquo modo sc. *interficeretur,* cp. Cat. II. 11 *quae sanari poterunt, quacunque ratione, sanabo,* v. R. 2289.

quis est qui puniendum putet, 'who thinks that punishment must necessarily follow?'   The subject of *puniendum* is perhaps the action implied in the clause *quoquo modo quis interfectus sit.*   Otherwise we must regard it as an impersonal gerund, as probably in § 19, *dolendum fuit sed certe puniendum nihilo minus fuit.*

C. IV.   **propinquus,** i.e. his nephew C. Lusius.

probus, like our own 'virtuous,' used specially in the sense of chaste.   Edd. quote Sall. Cat. 25 *saltare elegantius quam necesse est probae,* Hor. Ep. 17. 40 *tu pudica, tu proba,* cp. also Catullus 42. 24 *pudica et proba redde codicillos.*

perpeti turpiter, the adverb is unusual, but is used to make the antithesis to *facere periculose* more complete.

atque, 'and accordingly,' Näg. § 193.

ille summus vir.   Cicero always speaks of Marius in a very different way to the other democratic leaders.   Marius' undoubted services to the state, and the fact that he had opposed Saturninus, naturally weighed with him against his later career. Probably he had also a prejudice in his favour as an Arpinate, cp. Pro Sest. § 50 *divinum illum virum atque ex isdem quibus nos radicibus natum.*

scelere solutum, cp. § 31 *ut nos scelere solvamur.*

§ 10.   **volunt**, 'mean,' more often *sibi volunt.*

nata = *innata.*

arripuimus, hausimus, expressimus, ' caught up, sucked in, wrung out.'   All three words express *rapid* and therefore *instinctive* action contrasted with the slowness and passivity of the ordinary learner.

ad quam &c. 'which comes to us not by education, but by constitution, not by training, but by impression.'   In Orator § 165 Cicero quotes the sentence *est igitur—sumus* as an example of *concinnitas.*   This word sometimes means 'neatness,' sometimes 'rhythmical symmetry,' a quality which the passage undoubtedly has.   Yet it is by no means so clear and sharp as many of Cicero's less rhythmical antitheses: for (1) we cannot be *docti ad* anything, and the phrase must be explained as a zeugma: (2) *facti ad* is natural enough in such a phrase as *facti ad ludum et iocum* (De Off. I. § 103), but can we be said to be 'made for' the law of self-defence? (3) there is another zeugma in the second half; *instituti ad* is natural, but *imbuti ad* is not; (4) *imbuti* is not a very appropriate contrast to *instituti.*   It does not seem to be used of *instinctive* learning, but of *early* learning, whether natural or artificial.   Thus *imbui* gets two very different meanings: (*a*) (since knowledge acquired early is elementary), 'to get a slight tincture of.'   Cp. De Or. II. 162 (on which v. Wilkins) *doctrina liberaliter institutus et aliquo iam imbutus usu,* Tac. De Or. 19, *elementis studiorum etsi non instructus at certe imbutus*: (*b*) (because early impressions are best retained) to learn thoroughly, Cic. Phil. x. 10, 20 *ita a maioribus instituti atque imbuti.*

honesta, 'morally right' = *recte factum,* § 7 : predicate : the order of words *omnis honesta ratio* lays extra emphasis on *omnis.* Cp. *diligentiam nimiam nullam putabam,* § 66.

incidisset...esset.   The tenses following on the present *lex est* should be noticed.   In clauses depending on an historic tense the imperfect and pluperfect subj. are regularly used, though the effect spoken of belongs to the present, e.g. in § 34 *vos adepti estis ne quem civem metueretis,* v. Madv. § 383.   Here however we have the rule extended to cases where the principal verb is in the present.   The reason no doubt is that the law is thought of as made in the past.   So again in § 11 *vetat lex...*

ut iudicaretur. So also of a writer, *Chrysippus disputat aethera esse eum, quem homines Iovem appellarent,* De Nat. I. 39.

silent enim leges, compare the saying of Marius (Plut. Mar. 28) after illegally bestowing the citizenship, 'that he could not hear the laws for the din of arms,' and Lucan I. 277 *sed postquam bello leges siluere coactae.*

cum ei qui velit... 'when he who is willing to wait for legal protection must suffer injustice before he can get justice.' *repetenda,* by attraction for *repeti possit.*

§ 11. **etsi,** cp. *quamquam,* § 6.

persapienter, i.e. very cautiously and without encouraging homicide.

ipsa lex, an actual law ('the law' is *leges*), i.e. the *lex Cornelia de sicariis,* which ran *qui cum telo ambulaverit hominis necandi causa hominemve occiderit* &c.

quae non modo—The Cologne MS. followed by many editors omits *modo,* but there can be no doubt that the *lex Cornelia* ran as stated above. But, apart from this, the sense seems to me quite as good with *modo* as without. Cicero's argument is as follows. Had the law *only* said, *qui occiderit hominem,* it might have been taken to forbid homicide under any circumstances. But the words *causa occidendi hominis* limit the meaning of *occidere.* To say that it is unlawful to carry weapons for one purpose, implies that it is lawful to carry them for some other purpose. This lawful purpose must be that of self-defence. Therefore *causa hominis occidendi* must be taken as the opposite of *causa sui defendendi.* Therefore throughout the statute *occidere* must be understood to exclude cases where homicide is committed in self-defence. I do not see any 'fallacy' here. If the law sanctions a man carrying a revolver, surely it may be taken to imply that shooting with a revolver is in some cases justifiable.

iudicaretur—for the tense v. note on *esset,* § 10.

hoc maneat in causa. 'Let us consider this as settled in dealing with the case.' Cp. De Off. III. 49 *maneat ergo, quod turpe sit, id nunquam esse utile.*

C. v. § 12. **sequitur illud,** the decision of the senate was said by the Clodians to constitute a *praeiudicium,* against Milo (Quint. v. 2). *Praeiudicia* had always very great weight with a Roman jury, because, as Quintilian l.c. says, the jury are always inclined to uphold the decision of another jury, feeling that they may also require the same support, *refelluntur raro per contumeliam iudicum...confugiendum ergo ad aliquam dissimilitudinem causae.* This is of course just what C. does. For the importance which C. himself attached to *praeiudicia,* when it suited his purpose, v. the Pro Cluentio.

caedem in qua occisus est, a milder phrase than *caedem qua* which would have suggested wilful murder. *Occisus est* indicative, because C. does not profess to be quoting the exact words of what, according to the Clodians, had been decreed by the senate. But v. Introduction, page xxvi.

studiis, 'manifestations of approval,' cp. § 4.

summum, 'at the most.' The accusative is the same as in the ordinal adverbs *primum, tertium &c.* R. 1095.

huius, Munatius Plancus. C. says of him Ad Fam. vii. 2, *Oderam hunc multo peius quam illum ipsum Clodium.* Observe that throughout the speech he refuses to name him, cp. § 14.

ambusti, 'singed' i.e. by the flames of the burning senate-house on Jan. 19th. Some editors see an allusion to Plancus' 'blasted' reputation. Metaphors of burning are often used in connection with ruin and disgrace. A man who is utterly disgraced is said *conflagrare*, to be burned up (cp. § 75); a man who narrowly escapes is said to be *ambustus*, singed.

intermortuae, 'so nearly stifled' (or 'extinguished'), i.e. by the flames of the senate-house. The word *salse et acriter concioni tribuitur, quae repente flammis perculsa imminentibus, quasi extincta, ceciderit, tum postea revixerit iterumque viguerit*, Garatoni. But the exx. in the Lexicons do not give any clear authority for this sense of *inter-morior*, and it is opposed to the ordinary use of *inter-*, which adds force rather than limitation to a word like *morior*, cp. *inter-neco &c.* Can it not mean 'which fell so dead,' without any reference to the senate-house fiasco? C. might naturally hint that Munatius' agitation, whatever it might effect against M. was powerless against himself.

potentia, 'power' (from wealth or rank). *Auctoritas*, 'personal weight': *gratia* is the influence we have with those who like us or are grateful to us: 'popularity' is often the nearest English word. Cp. Caec. 73 *neque inflecti gratia neque perfringi potentia. Potentia* has often an invidious sense, cp. Cael. 22 *contra periculosas hominum potentias.*

in bonis causis, 'in recommending right or constitutional proposals.'

hos officiosos labores, 'my efforts to do my duty to them here' (in the law-court), i.e. my labours as an advocate on the constitutional side. *Officium* is frequently used in connection with an advocate. An advocate at Rome did not undertake a case 'professionally.' He was expected to have a good reason, which forced him to undertake it, as a matter of duty, cp. Quint. iv. 1, 7 *existimetur venisse ad agendum ductus vel officio cognationis vel amicitiae, maximeque, si poterit, rei publicae*, cp. also Pliny's letters vi. 29.

§ 13. hanc vero quaestionem, v. Introduction, page xiv. As opponents might argue that the existence of this special *quaestio* showed that the senate regarded M. as dangerous, C. shows in the next two sections, that the senate was really opposed to its establishment.

etsi non est iniqua. C. is anxious not to attack Pompey openly. For his (Cicero's) disapproval of the special commission, v. Phil. II. 22 *de morte Clodii fuit quaestio non satis prudenter illa quidem constituta: quid enim attinebat nova lege quaeri de eo, qui hominem occidisset, cum esset legibus quaestio constituta?*

erant enim leges, i.e. *Lex Cornelia de sicariis* or *Lex Plotia de vi.*

cuius enim &c. 'When Clodius committed his act of impious immorality, the senate had not been allowed to decide the method of trial. Who can suppose that they thought a new form of trial was required to investigate his death?' The reference is of course to the famous intrusion of Clodius into the rites of the *Bona Dea*, to prosecute, as was supposed, an intrigue with Caesar's wife. The intrigue constitutes the *stuprum*, the violation of religious rites the *incestum*, v. on § 59.

iudicium decernendi, 'of regulating the mode of trial.'

potestas esset erepta. The senate at first wished the judges to be chosen by the praetor. Ultimately however they were chosen by lot. In Atticus I. 16 Cicero attributes the break down of the prosecution to this.

incendium curiae, &c. v. Introduction, p. xii.

§ 14. illa defensio contra vim, 'the self-defence I upheld above' (in §§ 9, 10).

nisi vero, 'otherwise we shall have to suppose that, &c.' v. on § 8. The MSS. have *non* twice over, once before *etiamsi* and again before *vulnerarunt*. Both cannot be right and it seems best to omit the first. The difficulty of the sentence with this reading lies in the word *tamen*. Naturally it should mark a contrast between *etiamsi* &c. and *non vulnerarunt*. But these are similar, not dissimilar. We must suppose that C. feeling that the whole of the sentence, whose principal verb is *vulnerarunt*, amounts to a statement that these conflicts did damage the state, inserts the word *tamen* without thinking of the meaning of the particular words *non vulnerarunt*, if taken by themselves. Madvig proposed to omit the 'quo' before 'arma' and the *second* 'non.'

e re publica, 'in accordance with the public interests.' The sense of 'interest' lies in the *res*, not in the preposition.

C. vi. **decrevi**, 'voted,' of an individual senator: so not unfrequently in the Philippics e.g. xiii. 8 *honores ei decrevi quos potui amplissimos*, so *reservavi, notavi.* Below *decernebat* is not I think (as Edd.) 'was about to vote,' but 'was in process of voting.'

sed cum inesset &c., 'but since the affair involved violence and conspiracy to murder, I voted for denouncing it, while leaving the question where the guilt lay to be decided by a court of law.'

furiosum tribunum, Munatius Plancus.

ut veteribus legibus &c., i.e. that the case should be tried by existing laws and not under a special *quaestio*. At the same time the senate wished it to come on *extra ordinem* i.e. take precedence of other cases and be tried on what were usually holidays. It would appear from Ad Fam. viii. 8 that all cases *de vi* were taken *extra ordinem*, v. Tyrrell's note.

divisa sententia est, 'the motion was put in two parts.' The original motion was that the fray in the Appian road and the other acts of violence were dangerous to the state, and also that an *extra ordinem* enquiry should be held under existing laws. On the demand of Fufius Calenus the two parts of the motion were put separately. The first part was carried, the second vetoed by Munatius.

postulante nescio quo. Any senator might demand that a complex motion should be 'divided' by crying 'dīvĭdĕ.' The *nescio quis* is Fufius Calenus, who made the proposition finally accepted by the senate with regard to Clodius' trial. Cicero's attempt to ignore him must be only an affectation.

reliqua auctoritas. 'The rest of the resolution was invalidated.' *Auctoritas* is specially used of a decree which has been vetoed and thus prevented from becoming a *senatus consultum*. Cp. Ad Fam. viii. 8 where a number of such *senatus auctoritates* are given.

§ 15. **rogatione**, v. Introduction, pp. xiii, xxvi.

res, 'question of fact,' *causa* (here) 'question of guilt' = *crimen* above. A *res* becomes a *causa* when it involves some person's interests or character, cp. Pro Caec. § 11 *multa, quae sunt in re, quia remota sunt a causa, praetermittam.*

tulit enim sc. *ut quaereretur*. Distinguish between 'ferre ad populum' and 'referre ad senatum.'

nempe, cp. § 7.

paret, legal archaism for *apparet*.

in confessione facti &c. 'that avowal of the deed does not exclude the possibility of justification.' For this use of *ius* as opposed to *factum*, cp. § 31, 51 and De Fin. iv. 6 *quidquid* *quaeritur, aut facti, aut iuris, aut nominis, controversiam habet.*

quod nisi, 'but unless.' This *quod* (perhaps an old ablative, cp. *med=me, praedad=praeda*) is found also in the phrases *quod si, quod utinam, quod contra &c.*, v. R. § 536, Munro on Lucr. I. 82.

hanc litteram &c. 'The letter of mercy as well as that of doom' (Poynton). The two letters are A=*absolvo,* C=*condemno,* which were inscribed on the judges' tablets.

§ 16. iam illud &c. 'As to his reasons for the step, which he took upon his own initiative,—whether he regarded it as a concession due to the merits of Clodius, or to some special exigency—this no doubt he will explain himself.' *Iam* (as often *iam vero*) makes a transition to a fresh subject. C. has up till now been dealing with the terms of Pompey's motion: he now turns to another subject—why did Pompey propose a 'special' *quaestio* at all?

quod sua sponte fecit, i.e. in proposing a special *quaestio* Pompey acted without instruction from the senate. C. admits that the step requires explanation, but this he says P. will give himself, though he himself proposes an explanation in § 21. Meanwhile he gives reasons to show that it was not done in consideration of Cl.'s personal merits. *Illud* is not antecedent to *quod,* but is in apposition with the clause *Publione...tempori.*

C. VII. domi suae &c. C. now proceeds to give instances of Romans far greater than Clodius, who were murdered, and yet were not the subjects of special *quaestiones.*

atque illis quidem temporibus. 'Patron you might almost call him in those troublous times.' The word *patronus* implies the helplessness of the people protected more strongly than *propugnator.*

M. Drusus. Mommsen gives a somewhat different view of this 'Gracchus of the aristocracy.' Though a partizan of the senate, his schemes of reform were not congenial to the aristocracy, and he was finally deserted by them. In de Or. I. 24 C. again connects his cause with that of the senate.

nihil...populus consultus, *i.e. nulla rogatio ad populum lata est.* For the phrase cp. Livy IX. 22 *nihil consultus dictator. Nihil* is perhaps not an adverb but a second accusative after *consulo,* cp. Att. VII. 20 *nec te id consulo.*

cum P. Africano, 'on that famous occasion when Africanus fell a victim to a midnight murder.'

quem...mortem, 'that death was not even left to take its natural course with one for whom all would wish immortality, if it were possible.' Cp. Demosthenes de Cor. 205 περιμένειν

τὸν τῆς εἱμαρμένης καὶ αὐτόματον θάνατον, Cic. Phil. xii. 30 *mors
necessitatem fati habeat.*

§ 17.   quia non alio &c., 'the murder of the humble is as
heinous a crime as the murder of the great.'

vitae dignitatem, 'position during life.'

nisi forte erit.   The future, as often in English, is transferred from an actual to a logical consequence, cp. 'These two
triangles *shall* be equal' &c. in Euclid.   So Juv. i. 126 *noli
vexare : quiescet,* Don't disturb her : *you will find that* she is
asleep.

monumentis maiorum suorum, i.e. the Appia Via begun
by Appius Claudius Caecus in B.C. 312.   A public work or
building is often called the 'monument' of the magistrate
by whom it was made.   Cp. Hor. Odes, i. 2. 15, *monumenta
regis,* i.e. the buildings ascribed to Numa.   Sir C. Wren's
epitaph in S. Paul's *Si monumentum requiris, circumspice* illustrates this sense of the word.

maiorum, of *an* ancestor.   'Plural of appellative expressing
a *genus* where individuals are implied,' Kenn. 362.   Cp.
liberi=a child, Rosc. Am. § 96, Leg. Man. § 33.   In the use
of both these words the plural may be possibly due to the
fact that neither word can be used in the singular.   Mr
Poynton suggests an allusion also to the tombs of other Claudii,
which fringed the road.   This is possible (compare Juv.
v. 55 *monumenta Latinae* with id. viii. 146 *praeter maiorum
cineres atque ossa volucri carpento rapitur*) but not necessary.
monumentum and *monumenta* are interchangeable.

§ 18.   itaque, ironical, 'and therefore I suppose' (i.e.
because the Appian Road was intended for future Claudii to
commit outrages on).

nobilis, not, I think, ironical, as some edd., but in opposition to *equitem.*   The Clodians who complained of Cl. being
killed *in monumentis maiorum* are credited by C. with claiming
that a noble had special immunities.   It must be remembered
that only a noble could well have *monumenta maiorum.*   'They
saw no harm I suppose in Cl. killing Papirius, Cl. was a noble
in his own *monumenta,* and Papirius was only a knight.'
Perhaps we have here a touch of personal spleen from one
who was himself a *novus homo,* and an *eques.*

tragoedias, 'cant,' 'rhapsodies.'   Cp. de Or. i. 51. 219.

silebatur, 'was ignored.'

crebro usurpatur, 'continually brought up' (possibly with a
sense of using wrongly), v. Nettleship's Contributions to Latin
Lexicography, s.v.

parricidae, 'traitor,' 'assassin,' cp. Sall. Cat. 31. 8 *Catilinae obstrepere omnes hostem atque parricidam vocare.* v. Ramsay on Pro Clu. § 31.

imbuta, 'stained,' a milder word than *cruentata* (steeped), cp. Phil. xiv. 3. 6 *imbuti sanguine legionum gladii vel potius madefacti,* v. on § 10.

sed quid illa, *illa* does not refer to the last three sections which have been merely a digression, but to the cases of Africanus and Drusus. 'Why appeal to instances in the *past*?' v. on § 8.

comprehensus est, i.e. in b.c. 58, cp. Pro Sest. 69, Piso 28.

caruit, 'kept away from.' Cp. Ac. ii. 1, *caruit omnino rebus urbanis.*

non iure legum, cp. in Vat. 22, *cum non iure legum vel ianuae praesidio vita tegeretur. ius* here = 'lawful authority,' cp. *ius amicitiae* &c.

§ 19. **haec omnia,** i.e. *digna res, vir, tempus.*

summa fuerunt, 'were found in the highest degree,' cp. Pro Man. § 36 (speaking of the various virtues of a general), *summa omnia sunt in Pompeio.* Others take *summa* = 'of the highest importance.'

eo porro...tempore. Because Cicero was in exile, Cato in Cyprus, Caesar in Gaul.

proinde quasi &c., 'as if the law punished results not motives,' cp. Julius Paulus, v. 23 § 3 *qui hominem occidit, aliquando absolvitur, et qui non occidit, ut homicida damnatur, consilium enim unius cuiusque non factum puniendum est.*

puniendum, v. on § 9.

C. viii. § 20. **stulti qui audeamus,** 'fool that I am to venture,' R. 1714. The whole passage is of course ironical.

luget senatus &c., cp. (generally) Sest. § 32.

confecta senio, 'broken down.' Cp. Tusc. iii. 27, *Tarquinius dicitur senio et aegritudine esse confectus.* Notice the balance in the two halves of the sentence: in both we have verb, noun, verb, noun, noun, verb. Näg. § 167.

municipia, coloniae, so frequently coupled (sometimes the third kind of provincial towns, *praefectura* is added as e.g. Phil. ii. 58).

agri ipsi, cp. Verr. iii. 47, *ut ager ipse cultorem desiderare ac lugere dominum videretur.*

§ 21. In § 16 C. had said that Pompey could tell them whether the *Quaestio* was a tribute to Cl.'s personal merits, or

to a *tempus* or 'political necessity.' In the last five sections
he has shown the absurdity of the first alternative, and now
comes to the second. What then was the *tempus*? P. wished
to show regret for Cl. with whom he had lately been apparently
reconciled, but at the same time he felt sure that the jury
would acquit M. In fact he wished to appear M.'s enemy
without being so.

quadam, *quidam* is often used to apologize for, or qualify
an expression which may seem strange or inaccurate, v. Reid
on Pro Sulla, § 53. Compare also Näg. § 82 and Holden on
de Off. i. § 95, where a somewhat different view is taken. It
is not unfrequently coupled with *divinus,* cp. § 44 and Phil. iii.
3, *C. Caesar incredibili ac divina quadam mente praeditus.*
Here translate 'almost' or 'really.'

divina mente. Halm and others translate 'prophetic.'
But the common sense of 'godlike' suits better with *alta*
which = our 'lofty' rather than 'profound.' In this case, the
words convey an ironical reflection on P.'s meanness rather
than a genuine compliment to his sagacity. The policy
ascribed to him is obviously the reverse of 'lofty.'

ne videretur infirmior &c., 'lest the genuineness of the
reconciliation should be discredited.'

quamvis atrociter ipse tulisset, 'however severe was his
own motion.' An admission that Pompey's proposals argued
prima facie a belief in his guilt.

secrevit, 'set aside.'

non enim mea gratia &c., 'my influence is not limited to
the circle of my intimate friends.'

consuetudines victus, 'close and constant intercourse.'

res publica, cp. § 5.

fidem suam, *suam* is emphatic; had he not chosen *boni,* he
himself would have been no *bonus.*

§ 22. **iustitia,** 'power of judging justly,' **gravitas,** 'the
weight of character that will inspire respect,' **humanitas,** 'tact
and courtesy,' **fides,** 'the integrity that will withstand a bribe.'
Observe that we have *fides* here used for the third time in two
sections. The sense here differs from that of *fidem suam,* as
'integrity' does from 'honour.' An excellent account of the
meanings of *fides* will be found in Näg. 62.

tulit ut consularem necesse esset, sc. *quaestioni praeesse.*

principum, more frequently *principes civitatis,* also *in
re publica principes,* v. Reid on Sulla, § 3.

munus, a duty pertaining to a particular office or position.

temeritas, cp. § 2.

creavit. Domitius was actually *appointed* 'quaesitor' or 'president' of the court by the *comitia*, v. Asc. § 23. *Creavit* must refer to Pompey's influence.

populares, ' democratic.'

iam ab adulescentia, ' even from your youth.'

documenta maxima. According to Asconius this refers to the fact that Domitius when praetor in B.C. 58, broke up a meeting collected to agitate for the distribution of the *libertini* amongst all the tribes.

C. IX. § 23. Here we pass with a recapitulation of the *prooemium* to the *narratio*.

causam crimenque. Both words mean ' the real question to be tried.' But it is a *causa* to the judges, a *crimen* to the accuser and defendant, cp. Balb. § 2, Planc. § 17.

si neque omnis confessio, 'if avowal is not in every case unprecedented.'

facti, iuris, cp. § 15.

reliquum est ut quaerere debeatis, a slight pleonasm for *reliquum est ut quaeratis*, of the same type as the common *cogitate quid putetis faciendum*; cp. the still more pleonastic phrase *reliquum est ut de Catuli sententia dicendum esse videatur*, Leg. Man. 59, Zumpt 750.

uter utri. For the double interrogative cp. *decernere utri utris imperent*, Livy I. 23.

quod quo facilius argumentis &c. The proofs which will enable the jury to see the truth follow in § 32 &c., but to make these more intelligible, a *narratio* or statement of the facts (*res gesta*) is first given. *Perspicere ex argumentis* would be more usual than *perspicere argumentis*.

§ 24. **videretque** &c. Cl. had been Curule Aedile in 56, and would naturally have held the next highest office of Praetor in 53 (*annus suus*), the *Lex Villia* requiring that a magistrate should be out of office two years before holding another. The praetors for 53 should have been elected in 54, but as a matter of fact the election did not come on till half-way through 53. Clodius therefore determined to put off his candidature till the next year.

qui non spectaret, 'since his object was not advancement in rank.' Most people took office chiefly for the honour it conferred, and would not care how long they actually took power.

annum suum, i.e. the *earliest* year in which a man might legally hold a magistracy; cf. De Am. § 11 *Scipio factus est bis consul, primum ante tempus, iterum sibi suo tempore, rei publicae paene sero.*

religione aliqua, 'through some religious scruple.'

§ 25. **occurrebat,** 'the thought was continually suggesting itself' (Purton). Perhaps more accurately 'the counter thought' the *ob* in *occurro* having its full meaning as in § 48. The thought of having Milo as a colleague was an *objection* to his plan of transferring himself to the next year.

fieri, 'was in process of being appointed.' The appointment being determined by the canvassing as well as the election is regarded as beginning with the former.

convocabat tribus. The tribe was the organization on which a canvasser usually set to work. So we read of *spectacula* (seats at the games) and banquets given *tributim.* Cp. Quintus Cicero's letter to his brother 'de petitione Consulatus,' passim.

se interponebat, 'he made himself the go-between.' The corresponding substantive is *interpres.*

Collinam novam &c., 'he was registering a new Colline tribe,' i.e. he founded *sodalicia* or *collegia,* political organizations in which the members were registered (*conscripti*) and divided into bodies of 10 (*decuriae*). These organizations or one of them was composed according to C. of such *canaille,* that it might be called a new Colline tribe. The Colline was composed of the lowest class of citizens. For this use of *conscribere* and for the whole subject of these political organizations v. Holden's introduction to the Pro Plancio.

convalescebat, *convalesco* is more often used of growing strong after being ill or weak; but there is not the least reason to suppose with Mr Poynton that *misceo* here means 'to brew poison,' and *convalesco* 'to recover from the poison.' *Miscere omnia* is a well-known phrase for 'to create disturbance.'

sermonibus, 'by the voice of public opinion.'

suffragiis. The comitia had been held more than once, but had been interrupted. So far as the voting had gone, it had been in favour of M.

palam, 'publicly,' **aperte,** 'in plain terms.' Cp. Verr. Act. **I.** 18 *aperte palamque dicere.*

§ 26. **silvas publicas,** i.e. tracts of forest land, let out by the state to graziers. The rent paid was called *scriptura.*

ex Appennino, cp. fragment de Aer. Milonis II. 2, *eosdem ad caedem civium de Appennino deduxisti.* Edd. quote Phil. XII. 23, from which it appears that Cl. had estates on the *via Aurelia,* which runs along the sea coast of Etruria. But I do not see why we should suppose any allusion here to these estates. The natural inference from these words is that Cl. owned or rented pasture land on the Appennines and kept herdsmen there who made raids upon the other *silvae,* and also on the lowlands of Etruria. For the life of such shepherd slaves v. Mommsen, II. 184.

Note that the singular *Appenninus* is regularly used for the whole chain.

qua spe fureret. Not as Purton, 'what mad hope he was indulging,' but 'what aim he had in such violence.' The question of Favonius did not presuppose that the hopes of a *furiosus* were themselves mad. On the contrary it was taken for granted that the *furiosus* had some *bad* but *intelligible* object. Favonius could not imagine what it could be, while Milo remained alive.

summum, cp. § 12.

hunc, cp. § 16, *huius iudicis.*

C. x. § 27. sollemne, legitimum, 'prescribed by religion and law.'

ad flaminem prodendum, 'to nominate a flamen' (to Juno Sospita), *prodo* a technical word used of the appointment of a *flamen* and an *interrex.*

dictator Lanuvi. Both the Annian family into which M. had been adopted and the Papian to which he belonged by birth, traced their descent to Lanuvium. 'Dictator' was probably an ancient title of office at Lanuvium dating from its independent days, and now limited to religious duties.

re, 'the sequel.' We infer his *motive* from what actually happened.

ita profectus est, ut...relinqueret, 'his departure involved his leaving' (or perhaps 'absenting himself from,' v. next note).

illo ipso die. If C. is accurate, this must mean 'the very day of the murder,' not 'of Clodius' departure.' *Contionati sunt eo die* (i.e. *quo Cl. occisus est*) *ut ex actis apparet C. Sallustius et Q. Pompeius,* Asconius on § 45. But the accuracy of the rest of the narrative is not such as to inspire confidence that C. may not have made a mistake, or perhaps intentionally left the date ambiguous.

obire, 'to fail not.' Cp. De **Am.** 7 *obire diem et munus.*

§ 28. **calceos et vestimenta mutavit.** At the senate and on all public occasions Milo wore the *toga* and *calceus.* When he came home he would naturally take off the *toga* and change the *calcei* for *soleae* or 'slippers.' On this occasion he perhaps put on some other kind of *calcei* more suited for travelling than those worn at the senate (senators wore a special *calceus* which came higher up the leg and bore in front a crescent, v. Mayor on Juv. VII. 192). Instead of the *toga* he put on the *paenula,* a long thick sleeveless cape with only an opening for the head.

id temporis, for this phrase, in which the accusative of time 'during which' is loosely used for the ablative of time 'when,' v. R. 1088, 1082.

raeda or 'reda', for the bulkiness of the *reda* or family coach cp. Juv. III. 10 *dum tota domus reda componitur una,* and Martial, III. 47. 5.

Graecis comitibus. A common element in a great household sometimes for instruction, sometimes amusement. Greeks were selected on account of their *sermonis leporem, ingeniorum acumen, dicendi copiam,* Pro Flacco, 9, where Cicero allows them these qualities, but at the same time says that they had no sense of truth or honour. Compare also the well known description in the third satire of Juvenal.

hic insidiator. This is of course ironical.

apparasset, subjunctive of 'reported definition,' R. 1740.

paenulatus, for the *paenula* v. Mayor on Juv. v. 79. Here it is opposed to *expeditus* in the description of Clodius, cp. *paenula irretitus,* § 54, *paenulis astricti et veluti inclusi,* Tac. Dial. de Or. 39.

muliebri...comitatu. Wirz and Poynton take this as equal to *muliebri ancillarum et delicato puerorum comitatu,* but *muliebris* is then an unnecessary epithet; it seems better to say that both adjectives refer to both substantives and that *muliebris* means as usual 'of or belonging to a woman,' i.e. Milo's wife. Translate 'the feminine and feeble following of maids and pages.'

§ 29. **aut non multo secus.** For this and other questionable parts in the *narratio* v. Introduction.

cum telis, 'armed,' cp. *cum telo,* § 11.

adversi, 'in front.' Purton quotes *adversi dentes,* 'the front teeth.'

reiecta paenula, 'throwing his paenula back over the shoulders &c.'; the paenula had probably a slit beginning from the middle, v. the description in Rich. Mayor on

Juvenal, v. 79 infers from the phrases *paenula irretitus* and *astrictus* that it was a *close fitting* garment, but how then could it be thrown back?

quod putarent. An instance of the well known idiom by which the *verbum declarandi* or *sentiendi* is itself put into the subjunctive instead of the verb dependent on it. Cp. R. 1742 and 1756, and Mayor on Phil. II. 7, who quotes our own careless expression 'he went away, because he said it was late.'

ex quibus &c. Halm and Eberhard give *qui* (or the *qui* clause) as subject to *occisi sunt* and *fecerunt*, and therefore presumably make *ex quibus* dependent on *qui* (or rather on its suppressed antecedent). We must then translate 'of these, those who were loyal were partly killed' &c. This will imply that some of the slaves were not *fideli et praesenti animo*. But why should we not say that *ex* depends (as often) on *partim* used as a substantive, and that *partim* itself is subject to *occisi sunt* and (in the first instance) to *fecerunt*? Translate in this case 'of these (for they showed loyalty &c.) some were killed, others &c.' This seems to agree better with the statement in §§ 54, 57. In either case, of course, *servi Milonis* is an ungrammatical, but rhetorically useful insertion.

fecerunt id. 'A masterly euphemism,' Halm. It implies without any actual false statement, that Cl. was killed on the spot, instead of being merely wounded.

C. XI. § 30. vi victa vis, the alliterative use of *v* (*w*) is particularly common in Latin, cp. §§ 64, 85, and in other speeches, e.g. Sest. 59 *vivus, ut aiunt, et videns cum victu ac vestitu suo publicatus.* Perhaps there as here, the admixture of *p* (*potius oppressa*) heightens the effect, v. Munro, Lucretius, Introduction, p. 311.

nihil habeo quod defendam, 'I have no defence to offer.' A common use of 'defendo,' e.g. Clu. 101 *cum idem defenderet, quod Accius.*

doctis, here 'civilized' or 'educated' people opposed to *barbaris. gentibus,* 'mankind' opposed to beasts. For this use of *gentes* cp. the phrases *ubi gentium* &c. and perhaps *ius gentium.*

§ 31. optabilius fuit, 'it would have been more desirable.' For the indicative v. R. 1564. The apodosis, as R. says, lies in the infinitive *dare,* not in the *fuit,* which is independent of the condition. If put exactly, the sentence would run *si ita putasset, iugulum dedisset, nam hoc optabilius fuit.*

iugulari, the word is said to be particularly used of 'a judicial murder.' I do not think it is more than a very forcible and perhaps colloquial phrase for 'destroy,' sometimes used literally, sometimes metaphorically. It is true that C. often uses it of a man condemned in a law-court, but considering that so many of his speeches are directed to saving men from being condemned in a law-court, this is not very remarkable. That the word has no sense at any rate of 'injustice' in it is shown by Pro Quinctio, 51, *iugulare civem ne iure quidem quisquam bonus vult.* Translate ' to receive his death-blow from you, because he had not submitted to receive it from Cl.'

hoc ita sentit, a common redundancy, v. a number of instances in Mad. de Fin. II. 17.

ita et senatus rem &c., a repetition of the substance of sections 14, 15.

C. XII. **impune,** adv. for adj. (either *impunitus* or *impunitum*).

§ 32. **magnam causam,** a strong 'inducement' or 'motive,' a sense of *causa* usually followed by a genitive, but cp. Rosc. Am. 84 *causam tu nullam reperietis in Sext. Roscio, at ego in T. Roscio reperio.* Here the genitive *occidendi Milonis* is more or less supplied by the words *in Milonis morte.*

illud Cassianum, 'cui bono' fuerit. 'The maxim of Cassius, Always consider who gained by the crime.' Cf. Rosc. Am. 84 *L. Cassius ille quem populus Romanus verissimum et sapientem putabat, identidem in causis quaerere solebat, cui bono fuisset,* Phil. II. 35 *quod si quis usurpet illud Cassianum, ' cui bono fuerit' vide ne haereat.* It would be unnecessary to warn the student against taking *cui* to agree with *bono*, but for the fact that the phrase is so constantly misquoted. Mayor on Phil. II. 35 remarks that the Latin for 'what good is it to you ? ' is *quo tibi id ?*

in his personis, 'in the characters before us,' M. being a type of *bonus*, Cl. of *malus*. But v. Additional note.

etsi &c., i.e. the *Cassianum* is only a rough and crude test. In Rosc. Am. 84 C.'s comment is, *sic vita hominum est ut ad maleficium nemo conetur, sine spe atque emolumento, accedere.*

fraudem, 'crime.'

atqui connects the minor premiss in a syllogism with the major, v. instances in Lewis and Short and compare Victorinus's arrangement of this passage as a syllogism in note at beginning of § 34.

assequebatur = *assecuturus erat,* cp. *veniebat* § 43.

quo, sc. *consule.*

quibus si non, ' with whose connivance at any rate, if not

with their help, he hoped to have free play (*eludere*) in those
mad schemes which he had deliberately planned.' For this
absolute use of *eludo* cp. Cat. i. 1 *quamdiu iste furor eludet.*
The use may be traced perhaps to the transitive sense of 'foil.'
Thence we get 'mock at' and then absolutely 'swagger.' Cp.
Näg. § 116.

 cuperent, simply 'wish,' **vellent**, 'purpose.'

 § 33.   **vestrae peregrinantur aures?** 'are your ears gone
abroad?' Or perhaps 'are your ears as the ears of foreigners?'
A foreigner could be said *peregrinari* at Rome, and of course
such foreign visitors would be out of the way of hearing what
was going on. Cp. Pro Rab. Perd. § 28 *adeone hospes es
huiusce urbis ut haec nescias ut peregrinari in aliena civitate,
non in tua magistratum gerere videaris?* De Fin. iii. 40 *videris
philosophiae civitatem dare, quae quidem adhuc peregrinari
Romae videbatur.*

 inusturus, perhaps with an allusion to the branding of
slaves, the proposed Clodian laws being regarded as enslaving
the citizens, but metaphors from fire are so natural to Latin
writers, that we need hardly look for any such special allusion,
v. instances collected in Näg. § 134. The word is used of anything which makes a deep or painful impression, cp. § 99. In
Piso 30 we find *lex inusta per servos, incisa per vim, imposita
per latrocinium.*

 Sexte Clodi...legum vestrarum, cp. the Virgilian *vestras
Eure domas* and *vos o Calliope.* For *Sextus Clodius* v. Introd.,
page xxii.

 e domo, i.e. out of Cl.'s house, when the mob surrounded it
on the night of the murder.

 Palladium. The image of Pallas on which depended the
safety of the city which possessed it. Several cities claimed to
have *Palladia.* The most famous was the Trojan, which
according to the legend made familiar to us by Virgil was
taken by Ulysses and Diomede, but according to another was
brought to Italy by Aeneas and preserved in the temple of
Vesta. Thence it was once rescued by L. Metellus in a fire.
Cicero is probably alluding to this rescue.

 ut...posses, 'that if you should light on anyone to act as
tribune under your directions you might present him with it
(and a precious present it would be) to assist him in carrying
out his duties.' **instrumentum tribunatus**, 'the paraphernalia
of a tribune.' Cp. the philosophical use of *instrumenta vitae.
videlicet* and *praeclarum* are both, as often, ironical.

 et aspexit me &c., 'there, did you see? he looked at me
with just the same glare in his eyes &c.' C. pretends to be

suddenly frightened at a look in Sextus's eyes, and turns to
the jury with this exclamation. The words are quoted by
Quint. (IX. 2. 56) as a *brevior a re digressio.* For a possible
lacuna in the MSS. here v. Introd., page xxxiv.

lumen curiae, 'the burning and shining light of the senate
house.' The natural meaning of the words is 'the glory of the
senate house.' **C.** means 'the man who set the senate house
on fire.'

C. XIII. punitus es. The deponent is found once elsewhere in C.'s speeches, and twice in the philosophical writings
(v. Merguet).

imaginibus &c., all the regular concomitants of a funeral.
imagines, the wax-works representing the ancestors of the
deceased. **exequiae,** 'the train of mourners.' **pompa,** 'the
whole procession.' **laudatio,** 'the funeral oration.'

infelicissimis lignis. *Infelix* as applied to *lignum* has two
senses, (1) barren, (2) accursed. The second may probably
spring from the first, cp. Plin. H. N. xvi. § 108 *infelices autem
existimantur, damnataeque religione quae neque seruntur unquam neque fructum ferunt.* The *infelicia ligna* here are the
senate house benches.

semustilatum. C. uses the same taunt against Antony
with regard to Caesar's body, Phil. II. 91. So Suetonius of
Caligula.

laudare non possum &c., 'though I cannot praise, I certainly ought not to feel resentment.' The words *laudare non
possum* are really logically subordinate, v. on § 84.

§ 34. In regard to the text here it should be noted (1) that
the other MSS. go straight on from *debeo* to *P. Clodi praeturam,* and the words *fuerit...solutam* are only found in a leaf
of the Turin Palimpsest, (2) that the beginning of the sentence
audistis, iudices, quantum Clodi inter has been supplied by
conjecture, (3) that there is probably a further gap. The
rhetorician Victorinus describes this whole passage as a syllogism, in which we have

    (1) Major premiss,
        *si doceo causas fuisse Clodio, ut occideret M., probo
           insidiatorem.*
    (2) Minor premiss,
        habuit autem causas Clodius.
    (3) Conclusion,
        *quare si habuit causas Cl. ut occideret M., constat
           insidiatorem fuisse.*

It is supposed that this conclusion came in between *debeo*
and *audistis.*

non dicam admitteret, 'should ever be tempted, much less yield to the temptation.' The phrase brings out well the original meaning of *admittere* or *admittere in se.* "It expresses moral liability incurred freely, while *committere* designates the overt act punishable by civil law," L. and S.

sed, for *sed etiam* as in § 11.

fiebat. Halm compares the imperfect with *assequebatur,* § 32, but the force of the tense is somewhat different. *Assequebatur* expresses the hope or prospect of attainment. Here *fiebat* expresses that the process of becoming consul was actually going on, v. on *fieri* § 25.

sibi...proponeret, 'pictured to himself.'

solutam...fore. The past participle with 'fore' properly speaking makes a *future perfect inf.* R. 1369. But here 'solutam' is an adj. 'unshackled.' The epithet is in keeping with the name *belua* so often given to Clodius.

usitatis rebus. "The usual means of a candidate."

dignitatem, 'his position,' practically meaning his succession to the consulship: without this his political career would be spoilt and his position lowered.

cottidie augebatur, a breach of the well-known rule that 'cottidie' is used of daily *repetition* 'in dies' of daily *increase.* That Cicero did recognise this distinction appears from Att. v. 7, 1 *cottidie vel potius in dies singulos breviores litteras ad te mitto,* which Hand Tursellinus III. 342 explains to mean 'I send you letters which are shorter *than they used to be,* or rather they get shorter every day.' On the other hand it appears from Merguet's Lexicons that in the speeches and philosophical writings C. uses *in dies only* 7 times, always with a word of comparative force, *cottidie* frequently, *but also 7 times with a word of comparative force.* Thus De Sen. 50 *senescere se multa in dies addiscentem,* but id. 26 *cottidie aliquid addiscentem senem fieri,* De Fin. IV. 65 *hi levantur in dies: alter plus valet cottidie.* Professor Tyrrell on Att. I. 20, applies Hand's explanation to the passage *cottidie magis in his studiis conquiesco,* which he says means 'there is not a day but I feel my increased sense of recreation in literature,' while with *in dies* it would mean 'that sense becomes stronger and stronger every day.' This seems strained and at any rate no such distinction can be made with regard to the present passage, or to many of the others.

metueretis, for the tense v. note on *iudicaretur,* § 11.

exercitatio, 'means or scope for exercising.' Cp. De Sen. § 38 *hae sunt exercitationes ingenii, haec curricula mentis.* v. Näg.

§ 58, who quotes *omnem recusationem adimere Crasso volui*, De Or. II. 364, *habet res deliberationem*, Att. VII. 3.

suffragationem consulatus, 'a means of gaining votes for his appointment.'

mortuo denique, 'only after his death.' A use of *denique* frequent with *tum, nunc*. Here the word *mortuo* supplies the mark of time, cp. *hora decima denique*, § 48.

coeptus est temptari. The rule that *coepi* is used with an active infinitive, *coeptus sum* with a passive, appears to be absolutely maintained by Cicero. So also with *desino*, v. Zumpt, §§ 221, 200, Dräger, Hist. Syn. I. 93. The only exceptions *fieri* and *moveri* (*quod se ipsum movet nunquam ne moveri quidem desinit*, Tusc. I. 53) are obviously not real exceptions. Other writers are said not to be so particular: v. also Munro on Lucr. I. 1045, where he says that *quitur, potestur*, &c. are found in old writers where followed by a passive infinitive.

§ 35. **punitor**, 'avenger,' a rare word not found elsewhere in Cicero. *Punio* (or *punior*) is sometimes found in the sense of 'avenge.'

dolor, 'grievances.'

maxima, cp. *summa*, § 19.

segetem ac materiem gloriae, lit. 'the soil out of which his glory sprang, the material out of which it was made.' Mr Purton translates 'through whom he reaped glory, and achieved renown.' Cp. Livy VI. 7, 3 *hostis est quid aliud quam perpetua materia virtutis gloriaeque vestrae?*

praeter odium, 'beyond,' 'apart from,' cp. Leg. II. 43 *sceleris poena, praeter eos eventus qui sequuntur, per se maxima est*, but *praeterquam*, or *nisi odio*, would be more natural. *Praeter* usually couples two substantives, but compare such phrases as *victus est praeter opinionem*.

civile odium, 'political antipathy,' hatred felt on patriotic and not on personal grounds.

quo odimus. 'Cognate ablative,' R. 1099, cp. *Appius odisse plebem plusquam paterno odio*, Liv. II. 58.

ille erat ut odisset. 'As for Cl. he had a reason.' The *ille* is put in front for emphasis. Halm takes *erat ut* 'it was the case that,' but v. Zumpt, 562 and 752, where he distinguishes *est ut* = 'it is the case that' (most familiar to us in the phrase *fore ut*) from *est ut* = 'there is how' = *est cur*, or *est quod*.

lege Plotia, i.e. *de vi*, v. note on *in iudicium bis vocavit*, § 40.

quantum odium illius &c., 'How intense was his hatred, think you, how just even, for a man who had no justice in him?'

C. xiv. § 36. iam, 'still' or 'next.' We have the same position of *iam* in *reliquum est ut iam debeatis* in § 23.

natura ipsius consuetudoque, 'his personal character and life.' *ipsius*, because a man's character is regarded as being more a part of himself than his passions.

cessi, i.e. at his banishment in B.C. 58.

credo, as usual introducing an ironical statement, the reverse of the truth. Such irony is much commoner in Latin rhetoric than in English (except perhaps in the Artful Dodger in Oliver Twist). Such statements are often, I think, best translated, not by rendering *credo* by 'forsooth,' or any such word, but by putting the whole sentence in the form of a question. "Had he named a day? Had he proposed a fine? Had he brought an action for high treason?"

diem dixerat, i.e. if Clodius had acted legally, he would have (1) named a day for C.'s trial, which could only be done by a magistrate, (2) he would then have moved the infliction of a fine in the *comitia tributa* or (3) impeached him on the capital charge of *perduellio* (*intendere actionem perduellionis*) before the *comitia centuriata*.

perduellio, 'high treason'—the crime of being a public enemy (from *duellum* 'war' and *per* which stamps it with an unfavourable sense), a term which in Cicero's time was being rapidly supplanted by *maiestas*. Little distinction can be drawn between the two except that *maiestas* was tried before a *quaestio perpetua*, or jury court, *perduellio* before the people. For details and disputed points on the subject v. introduction and appendices to Heitland's edition of the Pro Rabirio.

et mihi videlicet &c., 'and I suppose I had reason to dread a verdict! my cause was not an excellent one, or one of public interest, but a bad one, or at any rate purely personal!'

iudicium, i.e. *iudicium populi*. C. implies throughout the whole passage that Cl.'s legal course was to bring him before the people, either in the centuries or the tribes. C. by executing the Catilinarians had offended (if at all) against the *lex Sempronia, ne de capite civium Romanorum iniussu populi iudicaretur*. The penalty for this was liability to trial before the people probably on a charge of *perduellio* (Heit. Pro Rab. p. 113). (It will be observed that C. does not consider the possibility of a trial for *maiestas* before the *quaestio perpetua* established to try the offence.) As a matter of fact Cl. brought in two bills, the first that any one who had killed a Roman citizen should be banished (possibly this was never enacted), (2) a bill expressly banishing C. by name.   In our passage C. simply ignores these proceedings.   In Pro Sest. 64, 65 he declares that the bill was illegal as being a *privilegium* and that he himself only yielded to it, for the same reasons as he states here, namely to avert civil commotion.

§ 37.   **cum mihi adesset,** 'when he was supporting me.' Hortensius was one of a deputation sent to the senate to petition against Cicero's banishment and was mobbed by Cl.'s rowdies.   *adesse* is the technical word of one who supports or countenances a friend on his trial.   Cp. Hor. Sat. I. 9, 38. In this sense no doubt Hortensius on this occasion *aderat Miloni.*   Hence the *hunc.*

C. Vibienus.   According to Asconius, a senator of this name was crushed to death in a crowd on the day after Clodius's death.   The two events can hardly be separated; and either Asc. or C. must have made a mistake.   Elsewhere in speaking of the attack upon Hortensius (Pro Dom. 54, Pro Sest. 27, cp. also Dio Cass. xxxviii. 16) C. does not mention Vibienus's death, and Halm thence concludes that the error is Cicero's.   Surely this is rather a strain on our belief in Asconius's infallibility.   Wirz suggests that the words are interpolated in Asc.

itaque, 'and so,' i.e. seeing that his outrages were tolerated.

intentata.   Possibly we should read *intenta* with the Cologne manuscript; the MSS. of Asconius have also *intenta. intento* lacks authority, and *intendo* is frequent Clark, page XLI. [but *intento* occurs in at least two other passages of Cicero, v. Lewis and Short].

Pompeio, v. § 18.

istam Appiam, *ista = quae a vobis usurpatur,* v. § 18.

monumentum sui nominis, *sui* as though *Clodius* not *sica* were the subject.

longo intervallo.   We hear little of Cl.'s violence from the beginning of 56 to the end of 53.

nuper quidem, *videtur mihi loqui de eo die quo Coss. Domitio et Messalla* (i.e. 53) *inter candidatorum Hypsaei et Milonis manus in sacra via pugnatum est.*   Asconius.   The *regia* or 'palace' of Numa was on the *Via Sacra.*

§ 38.   **quid simile Milonis?**   'What is there in M. like this?'

quantae quotiens occasiones &c.   Cp. Quint. VII. 2, 43 *post* *haec intuendum alio tempore et aliter facere vel facilius, vel securius potuerit, ut dicit Cicero pro Milone, enumerans plurimas occasiones, quibus ab eo Clodius occidi potuerit.*

potuitne, for *ne*=*nonne* v. Zumpt, 352.

cum domum defenderet. On Nov. 12th, 57 B.C.—an account of this attack is given by C. in Att. IV. 3.

Sestius, Fabricius. Tribunes B.C. 57—instrumental in C.'s recall. Sestius is the person whom C. defended against Cl. in the speech Pro Sestio. For the events alluded to here see § 79 and 75, 76 of that speech.

Caecilius. Praetor in 57, (*de oppugnata domo nusquam legi*, says Asconius).

illo die cum est lata. Aug. 4th, B.C. 57. *lata*='proposed' not 'carried.'

totius Italiae concursus. 'All Italy assembled in her thousands.'

mea salus. 'The news of my restoration,' Purton. Rather 'the desire for my restoration (or deliverance).' The multitude came to *vote* for C.'s *salus* in the *comitia*. Cp. *ut ad me restituendum concurrerent*, § 39.

vindicaret. The subjunctive has to do double duty, being both consecutive and hypothetical. The more regular construction would be *vindicatura fuerit* (R. 1521, note at bottom of page).

C. xv. § 39. **at quod erat tempus!** exclamatory, not interrogative. "What an opportunity that was!" C. proceeds to dilate on the opportunities afforded for the murder of Cl. by the reaction against him in the year 57.

septem praetores (out of 8), **octo tribuni** (out of 10). The names will be found in the speech In senatum § 22.

gravissimam, 'powerful' (of the substance), **ornatissimam,** 'eloquent' (of the language).

cohortatus est, i.e. in a *contio*, Pro Sest. § 107.

decretum, i.e. as *duumvir* or chief magistrate of Capua. Pompey did not of course properly speaking pass the decree. The Capuan senate passed it, *Pompeio referente.* Cp. In Pisonem § 25.

cum...fecit, dedit, 'passed a resolution, and *thereby* gave.' The indicative with *cum* marks identity of action in the two verbs. This construction is generally found when the tense and person of the two verbs are the same. R. 1729.

eius, for *suam*, because *imploranti*=*cum imploraret*, in which case *eius* would be regular, Kennedy 234. Cp. Pro

Sulla 81 *adfuit post ad eum delatam coniurationem*, where *eum* refers to the subject of *adfuit*, Brutus 220 *Curius orator, vivis eius aequalibus, proximus optimis numerabatur.*

fidem, 'help.'

concurrerent, perhaps read *concurreret.*

quem qui tum interemisset, *quem qui = ut si quis eum.*

§ 40. in iudicium bis vocavit. Of these two prosecutions the best known is the second. M. summoned Cl. under the *lex Plotia* at the end of 57 B.C. for attacking his house. (The prosecution has already been alluded to in § 35, and the outrage in 38.) The case was never actually tried, through Cl.'s election to the *aedileship.* Of the 1st prosecution we have no direct account, but it is alluded to (1) in Att. IV. 3 *etenim antea cum iudicium nolebat, habebat ille quidem difficilem manifestamque causam, sed tamen causam, poterat infitiari, poterat in alios derivare, poterat etiam aliquid iure defendere.* (2) In the speech In senatum § 19, *M. primo Cl. de vi postulabat. Postea quam ab eodem iudicia sublata esse vidit ne ille omnia vi posset efficere curavit.* Of these two versions, we may safely take the first and infer that (1) Cl. was never actually brought to trial, and that (2) the reason of this was, that there was little or no case against him.

ad vim, 'twice to a trial of law, but never to a trial of force.'

reo ad populum. At the end of 56 Milo gave up his tribuneship and Cl. became aedile. He retaliated on M. by a counter prosecution (*de vi, quod gladiatores adhibuisset, ut rogationem posset de Cicerone perferre*). He prosecuted him before the people, instead of by the *lex Plotia*, possibly because there were at the beginning of the year no *iudices* owing to the postponement of the election of magistrates (v. Holden Pro Sest. Int. XXVII.). A graphic account of the proceedings is given in the letter Ad Quint. fr. II. 3. The prosecution was dropped.

cum in Cn. Pompeium. Cp. Ad Fam. I. 5 b *Posteaquam Pompeius apud populum cum pro Milone diceret clamore convitioque iactatus est...visus est mihi vehementer esse perturbatus.* There was no actual *impetus* however. The riot began after Pompey had finished. v. Ad Quint. fr. II. 3.

nuper, i.e. in 53. Antonius (the future triumvir) was sent by Caesar from Gaul to stand for the quaestorship. He brought letters of recommendation to Cicero, who supported him.

gravissimam partem rei publicae, 'a most important public duty,' i.e. *defensio bonorum.* Halm.

cum se ille fugiens &c. Phil. II. 21 *P. Clodium meo con-*

silio interfectum esse dixisti. Quidnam homines putarent si tum occisus esset, cum tu illum in foro, inspectante populo Romano, gladio insecutus es, negotiumque transegisses, nisi ille in scalas tabernae librariae se coniecisset hisque oppilatis impetum tuum compressisset? For *scalae* cp. Hor. Ep. II. 2. 14 (of a runaway slave) *ut fit in scalis latuit.* The space under the staircase was formed into a room or closet with a door to it, and was often used as a hiding-place. In a fragment of Cicero we find *opposuit fores scalarum.*

magnum fuit, 'was it a great matter?' Cp. Pro Planc. § 86 *decertare mihi ferro magnum fuit.* Pro Deiot. 19.

§ 41. **comitiis,** 'at the comitia,' i.e. for election of consuls for 52. The ablative without *in* is found with several nouns which, properly denoting events, have come to be used as marks of time, so *ludis, gladiatoribus, Saturnalibus.* Madv. 275, obs. 2.

campo, the *campus Martius* which bordered on the Tiber.

quotiens, because several attempts were made to hold the election, cp. *saepe* § 25. These particular circumstances probably belong to only one of these occasions.

saepta, 'pens' or enclosures in which the centuries were arranged at the *comitia.*

C. XVI. **querella,** the double 'l' should be used with words where the 'e' is naturally short, as it is with nouns formed direct from verbs of the 3rd conjugation, e.g. *luella, sequella, loquella.* On the other hand write *suadela, tutela, corruptela,* v. Lachmann (quoted by Mayor, Phil. II. 6).

§ 42. **honoris contentio.** Observe the use of the objective genitive, though the verbal noun does not represent a transitive verb, v. Madv. § 282, obs. 3, who quotes *vacatio militiae, fiducia virium;* cp. also *dimicatio capitis,* § 100.

ambitio, 'the position of a candidate.' The word sometimes denotes the feelings or character of the office-seeker; sometimes the exertions which he has to make to win the favour of the electors. It is of course wrong to translate by 'ambition' simply, but I am not sure that 'political ambition' is not the best translation in the majority of cases, though the word gets a special colour from C.'s habit of contemplating office as a *beneficium populi Romani,* to be gained not by showing merit, but by winning favour.

rumorem, any report, any tale however false, fictitious and worthless. *falsam* is simply 'untrue,' *fictam* suggests *deliberate* invention. Cp. *falsa atque insidiose ficta* § 67. There is a good deal of confusion in the MSS. here, v. Clark p. XLV. For 'fabula' in the sense of 'current gossip' cp. Caelius in Ad

Fam. VIII. 1 *omnia sunt ibi, senatus consulta, edicta, fabulae, rumores.*

molle...tenerum, 'fragile, delicate': so language (*oratio*) is said to be *mollis et tenera et flexibilis*, Orator § 52, cp. De Or. III. 176 *nihil est tam tenerum neque tam flexibile, neque quod tam facile sequatur quocumque ducas, quam oratio.* For the thought compare Pro Mur. § 35 where the 'working of the elections' (*ratio comitiorum*) is said to be more unstable than the tide in the Euripus.

fastidiunt, 'are captious and critical.' *fastidium* is an aversion to something which is naturally pleasant—so often coupled with *satietas.* Eberhard quotes the story of Aristides and the Athenian voter.

§ 43. **diem campi,** 'the day of election.' *Campus pro comitiis* is quoted De Or. III. 167 as an instance of *metonymy*, like *Mars* for *bellum* &c.

sibi proponens, 'with the prospect before him.'

ad illa augusta &c., 'did he mean to come to those solemn rites that introduce the meeting of the centuries?' For the imperfect cp. *assequebatur,* § 32.

quid? quod caput est &c. 'Again (and this is the main source of crime) who does not know that the greatest temptation to sin is the hope of impunity?' This must be the meaning of the reading and punctuation in the text. But the words *quod caput est audaciae* are then tautological. Others place the comma at *est* and take *audaciae* (=*audacibus*) as dative after *spem.* Others omit *audaciae.* With both these readings *quod caput est*='and this is the main point,' cp. § 83.

necessarii. C. begs the question in a curiously barefaced way. The main object of the speech is to prove that the act was *necessarium.*

contempserat. Halm translates 'had *always* despised,' but this is not necessary, v. on § 74.

fas as usual, used in relation to divine law (here identified, as by the Stoics, with nature). **leges,** human law. It should be remembered that *licet per leges* does not quite mean 'the law permits positively' (*legibus fieri licet*), but 'the law does not forbid.' *per*='without hindrance from.' R. 2037.

§ 44. **vos ex M. Favonio,** v. § 26.

vivo Clodio, i.e. while Clodius could contradict the story, if false.

post diem tertium quam dixerat, 'three days after he had said it,' v. Madv. § 276, obs. 6. And compare the familiar *ante diem tertium Nonas* &c. Of course, *quam* is a conjunction (as in *postquam*), not relative.

§ 45.   **quem ad modum** &c. 'How was it he hit upon the right day?' Cp. Cat. I. 7 *Num me fefellit non modo res tanta, verum, id quod multo magis est admirandum, dies.*

dixi modo, cp. § 27.

nihil negotii erat, 'it was no trouble.'

at quo die ? v. note on *illo ipso die*, § 27.

mercennario (not *mercenarius*; the original form is *mercednarius*), i.e. Sallustius or Pompeius—both of whom addressed the meeting (Asconius thought it was the latter to whom C. alludes here).

concitata, 'whose passions were inflamed,' Purton. If this is right cp. § 2 *concitatae multitudinis*. But it is simpler to translate 'brought together,' as in § 38 *quem mea salus concitarat.*

cogitatum facinus, cp. *cogitati furores*, § 32.

ne causa quidem, 'not even a pretext.' But C. ignores the fact attested by Asconius that Cl. had been attending a meeting of the town council (*decuriones*) of Aricia.

quid si, said with an air of triumph to introduce a clenching argument.

ut, 'while,' **sic** 'on the other hand.' So again in § 49.

scivit. Distinguish *sciebat* 'knew' from *scivit* 'came to know,' 'learnt.' So *scitum est* means 'information arrived.' Cp. Rosc. Am. 97 *qui tum cito scivit?* and *nondum lucebat, cum Ameriae scitum est.* So *scire* in the next section is the inf. of *scivit* not of *sciebat*.

§ 46.   **ut rogasset**, 'even though he had asked.'

illo ipso die. Another inaccuracy according to Asconius § 4 *profectus est ad flaminem prodendum postera die.*

[omnes scilicet Lanuvini]. An obvious gloss, first expelled by Lambinus.

quaesierit...corruperit. 'Grant that he asked...that he bribed.'

videte quid largiar, 'see what a liberal concession I make.' In the same sense *Plus ego largiar* Pro Caec. 35.

Interamnas. This appears to be the proper form for an inhabitant of Interamna. But the best MSS. (followed by most editions) have *Interamnanus*.

comes, i.e. upon this particular journey.

cuius iam pridem testimonio, 'the man whose testimony years ago made Cl. be at Rome and Interamna at the same hour.' When tried for violating the rites of the *Bona Dea* in 61, Clodius had called Causinius to swear that he was at Interamna (80 miles from Rome) at the time.

Albano, Purton says 'sc. *agro*,' but why not *praedio* as usual? ' in his *place* at Alba.'

comes item, 'also a companion' (as well as *some-one* else), **idem comes,** 'also a companion' (as well as *some-thing* else).

C. Clodius, a ' *de plebe notus homo*' according to Asconius, not the brother of Publius of that name.

C. xviii. § 47. **quantae res confectae sint,** ' what important results are established.'

liberatur non eo consilio profectus esse. M. 'is acquitted of having set out with the design.' *Liberor* is constructed as if it meant 'prove.' The commentators quote Phil. v. 14 *excusetur Areopagites esse,* and De Inv. ii. 98 *reus id quod fecerit fecisse defenditur,* but the usage in this passage seems to me far more remarkable. *Defendo eum fecisse,* 'I maintain that he did it,' is fairly common, e.g. Pro Mur. §5: so also *excuso eum Areopagitem esse* would be possible; and these imply the possibility of *defenditur fecisse, excusatur esse,* just as *dicunt eum fecisse* implies the possibility of *dicitur fecisse.* But we could not say *libero Milonem non profectum esse,* 'I prove that Milo did not go.' The Greek ἀπολύεται μὴ ἀδικεῖν ' he is acquitted of guilt' has certainly a *prima facie* resemblance; but there the infinitive is consecutive, a usage quite foreign to Latin. Is it possible that C. is intentionally imitating it?

quippe si &c., 'undoubtedly if the two were not to meet at all' (as would be the case if Cl. meant to stop in his Alban villa). *Quippe* is often thus used as a strong affirmative implying that any doubt is absurd. A number of instances are collected by Holden Pro Planc. § 53.

deinde. We should expect *ego quoque liberor;* instead we have the thought expanded in the words *scitis—liberatus sum.*

meum agam negotium, 'do myself a good turn.'

in suadenda hac rogatione, 'in advocating this bill,' i.e. the lex Pompeia, v. § 15: so *suadere legem,* Leg. Ag. ii. 101.

fuisse qui dicerent. Asconius on this place says the persons alluded to are Pompeius Rufus and Sallustius. In intr. § 22 he says that Munatius threatened C. with a *iudicium populi*: acc. to Dion 46. 2 Fufius Calenus made the same charge. In the face of this it is extraordinary that

Cicero in Phil. II. 22 should say to Antony *P. Clodium meo consilio interfectum esse dixisti...quod igitur, cum res agebatur, nemo in me dixit, id tot annis post tu es inventus qui diceres.*

alicuius. At first sight we might expect *cuiusdam,* the word used for a person who is definitely known, but for some reason is not named. *Alicuius* however is really more forcible; it represents the vagueness and mock caution which C.'s accusers would naturally adopt.

videlicet, explanatory of *alicuius,* not ironical as in §§ 33, 36.

describebant, 'portrayed,' often used in a bad sense, cp. Piso 68 *contumeliae causa describere:* so in Horace for *lampoon,* Sat. I. 4. 3.

iacent suis testibus, 'they are refuted (floored) by their own witnesses.' Observe that *a* is nearly always omitted by C. before *testibus,* when the effect produced by the witnesses on the case is described. A witness is rightly regarded as an instrument and not an agent; so far as he speaks the truth, his influence on the case is involuntary. On the other hand in such a phrase as *hoc dicitur a testibus,* the *a* could not possibly be omitted.

[11]. As the sense requires that *qui* should refer to *testibus,* not to the subject of *iacent, ii* (al. *hi*) must be omitted, or possibly the words *qui—rediturum* are a gloss. Clark p. XLIII.

cogitasse, 'to make a subject of reflection,' 'to base plans upon.'

§ 48.   **occurrit illud,** 'I am met by this objection,' v. on § 25.

ne Clodius quidem, 'neither Clodius.' *Ne quidem* like οὐδὲ is often used when there is no gradation, v. Mayor on Phil. II. § 10.

si quidem &c.   'Yes that would have been the case, if he had not intended to leave the house to commit the murder (but he did so intend), for I am sure that the person who is said &c. &c.' *Exiturus fuisset* is said by Halm to be a very rare use. The construction however is perfectly regular: *si facturus fuit, peccavit* is as regular as *si fecit peccavit,* and therefore *si facturus fuisset peccavisset* as *si fecisset peccavisset.* The rareness is probably due to the nature of the thought. The argument, 'if *A* did this *B* would have resulted, but *A* did not do it, therefore *B* did not result,' is practically far more common than 'if *A* intended to do this *B* would have resulted, but *A* did not *intend* it, therefore *B* did not result.'

video, 'I can see plainly,' 'I know well enough.' The use of *video* is far less restricted than that of the English 'see.'

obsignavi, 'sealed' i.e. 'witnessed.' The witness sealed the tape (*linum*) which bound the will, and wrote his signature by the side of it.

palam fecerat, cp. Phil. II. § 41 *quem palam heredem semper factitarat.* On both these passages Halm quotes Ulpian in Dig. 28. 1. 21, the upshot of which is, that a will may either be written or nuncupative i.e. oral, but that if oral it must be made *palam*, that is audibly, and before witnesses. If *palam* has the same meaning here, C. must mean that Cyrus made his will in both ways. (Mr Poynton says that *scripserat = nuncupaverat*, and that Cyrus did *not* make a will. How then did Cicero seal it?) I cannot see why *palam* in either passage of Cicero should mean more than 'without concealment.' Cyrus might have kept the contents of the will a secret from the witnesses. As a matter of fact, he did not do so, and therefore Clodius could not plead curiosity to hear the contents of the will as an excuse for returning to Rome.

eum nuntiabatur mortuum esse. *Mortuus nuntiabatur* is perhaps more regular (cp. § 66), but the impersonal construction is said to be more common with *nuntiatur* than with *dicitur*, particularly when followed by a dative. Zumpt 607. Madv. 400.

hora decima denique, 'only at the tenth hour,' v. note on *mortuo denique*, § 34.

C. XIX. § 49. age, 'well,' here used concessively as in Acad. II. 135 *Age haec probabilia sint; num etiam* &c.: more often to mark a transition as in §§ 55 and 60. According to Reid on De Sen. § 24 it is short for *hoc age* 'attend to this.'

coniceret se in noctem, 'plunge into the perils of the night,' Purton.

ecquid afferebat festinationis. Apparently the meaning is, 'did the fact that he was heir give a reason for hurrying?' But I can find no other instance where *adfero* is used with an abstract noun denoting *action*; though such phrases as *adferre metum, dubitationem* &c. are common enough. Probably C. has coined the phrase as the opposite of *adferre moram.*

festinationis)(properare. The distinction made by Cato (quoted Aul. Gell. 16. 14 and elsewhere), *aliud est properare, aliud festinare: qui unum quid mature transigit, is properat; qui multa simul incipit neque perficit, is festinat,* hardly applies here. Compare *cum omni festinatione properare in patriam,* Ad Fam. XII. 25. 3. If any distinction is to be drawn between the words, it must be that *propero* denotes the journey itself; *festinatio* the hurried preparations and actions incidental to a quick journey.

properato opus, 'need of haste,' a common construction in Sallust and Livy, but comparatively rare in Cicero. The employment of the passive participle used impersonally for a verbal substantive is in older Latin confined to this use with *opus* and *usus*. In Livy it is fairly common, as *degeneratum* 'his degeneracy,' *propter lapidatum* 'because it had rained stones.' In Cicero we find it rarely with *opus* as *opus quaesito* 'need of making money' Paradoxa 46. Otherwise probably only once, Partit. Or. 114, where in a list of the evidences of guilt we find *cruor telum pallor tremor haesitatum titubatum,* 'hesitation and embarrassment.' The use of the participle with a substantive to designate an abstract idea is much more common in Cicero. Thus *opus Hirtio convento, post Hirtium conventum,* cp. § 8 of this speech *de homine occiso,* v. Dräger, Historic Syntax § 575.

ut...sic, v. on § 45.

cum, ironically used for *si,* cp. *hic insidiator* § 28.

§ 50. Some MSS. insert after *exspectandum fuit,* "*noctu occidisset; insidioso et pleno latronum in loco occidisset.*"

salvum, 'acquitted,' so continually *salus.*

sustinuisset crimen locus, 'the brunt of the charge would have fallen upon the place,' &c.

occultator et receptor. For the verbal substantives in *-tor* and *-trix,* used almost as adjectives, sometimes denoting habit (as here), sometimes single actions, v. Näg. 54. Cp. *sica paene deletrix imperii,* De Har. 49.

locus, 'the locality,' i.e. the Appian road near Rome; the worst place seems to have been a certain *monumentum* or *bustum Basili* (Asconius on this place).

deinde ibi, if strictly and prosaically expressed, *ibi=si ibi occisus esset.* The abbreviation seems to me natural enough. The public is conceived of as finding Cl.'s body, and forming their suspicions on the spot. Suspicion would fall first on the thieves of the place, secondly on those who had suffered bodily violence, or had been threatened with it from Cl., thirdly on the Etruscans as a body, who had suffered so much from his slaves, § 26. The different tenses *sustinuisset, caderent, citaretur* serve to emphasise the fact that the thieves would be suspected first, and the outraged people only second. To take *ibi* with *spoliati* makes very poor sense. Why should those who had been maltreated by Cl. *there* be suspected more than those who had been maltreated elsewhere?

§ 51. **atqui,** some read *atque.*

certe, 'this is not a matter of conjecture.' The word

contrasts the admitted fact mentioned with the suppositions and disputed statements of the last few sections.

quod ut, 'now even though,' the *quod* is the same as in *quod si, quod nisi,* cp. § 15.

venturus esset, hypothetical subjunctive, 'to which he would be sure to come' (i.e. *si non in villa resideret*), or else virtually suboblique, 'to which *he thought* Cl. would come.'

video, 'I find.'

constare, 'are consistent,' 'point in one direction.'

§ 52. **nihil umquam auditum ex Milone.** This is shewn to be untrue by C. himself, Att. iv. 3 *si Clodius se obtulerit, occisum iri ab ipso Milone video. Non dubitat facere, prae se fert, casum illum nostrum non extimescit.*

exiturum, for the omission of *se* v. Zumpt 604, Mad. 401, Mayor on Phil. ii. 49 and Reid on Acad. i. 18. It is most common apparently when the infinitive depends, as here, on another infinitive with the same subject. The *esse,* as here, is usually left out.

C. xx. § 53. **id quod caput est,** 'which is the principal point.' Cp. § 43, Quint. v. 10. 37 *ducuntur argumenta et ex loco...quam partem videmus vehementissime pro Milone tractasse Ciceronem.*

ille ipse, 'where they actually did meet,' as opposed to the places where they *might* have met, §§ 50, 51. Or perhaps = *loci natura,* 'the ground,' as opposed to the other features of the meeting.

tandem, occasionally found in indirect questions (e.g. Clu. 123 *videamus quid tandem iudicasse videantur*), though by no means so frequently as in the direct.

vero, ironical. Cp. Livy ix. 17. 15 and 18. 6 *id vero periculum erat.* There is no need to put a mark of interrogation after *est.*

insanas, just as various buildings in England are called 'So and so's Folly.'

substructiones, cp. § 85. 'Clodius was building upon the side of the Alban Hill : after cutting back into the hill, and raising the lower ground, he would erect pillars on which would rest the ground floor of his house.' Poynton. Cp. Sall. Cat. 13. 1 *a privatis compluribus subversos montes.* The words *facile versabantur* &c., however, seem to me most naturally to imply that workmen were actually employed on the *substructiones* at the time. If so, since the house was built already (v. *egredientem e villa* § 54), they must have served some other purpose.

facile. I should prefer to say that the word goes with *versabantur*, rather than with *mille*: so too with the other instance quoted Verr. II. 35 *hereditas facile ad H. S. triciens venit.* The use of *facile* with adjectives seems in C. to be confined to superlatives or quasi-superlatives.

versabantur, so Müller reads, following the MSS. Most editions follow Aulus Gellius I. 16, 15 who quotes this passage and says that he found the plural in *libris minus accurate scriptis.* *Mille* with the genitive is found according to Roby § 1305, sometimes in Cicero, not unfrequently in Livy and Plautus, but rarely elsewhere. The instances where it is found as subject to a verb, are naturally still rarer, but it appears that the verb may be either singular or plural (v. Dräger I. § 57. 106).

edito atque excelso adversarii loco, either abl. of comparison or abl. abs.

spe ipsius loci. 'The ground was the *very* thing he relied on.' We may translate by transferring the emphasis conveyed in *ipsius* to some other word, 'who just because he relied on the ground, had planned to make the attack there.'

§ 54. The whole section is a good instance of the rhetorical device of ἐνάργεια or pictorial description: cp. Orator 139 *saepe rem dicendo subiciet oculis* and v. note on § 6.

gesta, 'in a statement of fact.' *Gesta* is an odd antithesis to *picta.* The implication is, that words are used to state fact, painting only to represent fiction.

inpeditissimum, 'very embarrassing,' a frequent meaning of the word. It is hardly true to say that the passive is used in an active sense. The explanation of the apparent change of voice lies in the meaning of the word itself. *quod impeditur impedit.* A thing which cannot be moved easily, prevents other people from moving. So with *expeditus.*

vehiculum. Any *vehiculum* was more cumbersome than a horse, and the *reda* was more so than other vehicles.

quid minus promptum. 'Could anything be less like a state of preparation for battle?'

paenula inretitus, v. § 29.

uxore paene constrictus. Observe the absence of the *ab.* His wife was the chain, not the chainer. 'Tied to the spot by his wife' will serve as a translation, as no one is likely to suppose that she actually strapped him down. Poynton translates 'by his wife's presence.'

videte nunc illum. Here begins the other side of the picture answering to *cum alter veheretur.*

tarde. There is no real contradiction between this and *properare* in § 49. The hurry referred to there consisted in his starting at such an unnatural time : so here *subito*.

qui convenit. 'What was the sense of that?'

Alsiensi, sc. *praedio*. Pompey is known to have had a villa at Alsium, which is on the coast of Etruria.

morae et tergiversationes, '*repeated* delay and shuffling.' But Halm and others read *mora et tergiversatio*, which is also the reading of the Cologne MS. The other MSS. have *morae et tergiversationis.*

C. xxi. § 55. **age nunc**, v. on § 42. The word has become so mere an interjection, as to be used with a plural imperative.

iter, 'mode of travelling.'

Graeculi, v. on § 28. The contemptuous diminutive is very common, e.g. the well known *omnia novit Graeculus esuriens; in caelum iusseris ibit* of Juvenal (3, 78). Compare the 'Bailie' in Rob Roy, 'We are bits of Glasgow bodies.'

etiam cum in castra Etrusca properabat. According to Asconius C. alludes to a story, that Cl. had set out from Rome to join the camp of the Catilinarians at Faesulae and then returned. It may be safely said that without this statement of Asconius every reader would without hesitation have referred the words to Cl.'s depredations of Etruria (v. § 26, and still more, 74 *non solum Etruscos...pellere possessionibus armis castrisque conatus est*). As it is, we cannot regard his opinion as decisive, though possibly he may have had further knowledge which enabled him to identify the allusion. The absurdity of Cl.'s retinue may have been an essential part of the story, as the tame eagle is an essential part of Napoleon III.'s expedition to Boulogne.

nugarum. L. and S. give 'jesters,' 'droll fellows.' Rather (as Tyrrell on Att. vi. 1. 15) 'nothing that did not mean business.' So too *nugarum aliquid*, Att. vi. 3. 2.

symphoniacos, 'choristers.' As to whether they played as well as sang, v. Dict. of Ant. s.v.

uxoris. It is essential to C.'s description of Milo, that such an effeminate retinue was his *wife's* not his own. So too *casu.*

qui duceret, 'the sort of man who always took.'

nisi ut, short for *nisi tales ut.*

virum a viro lectum, 'that each man had picked another.' Cp. Livy x. 38 *decem nominati sunt ab imperatore; iis dictum* *ut vir virum legeret, donec sedecim milium numerum confecissent*, i.e. the ten men choose another ten, these ten choose another ten, and so on. The idea of course is, that individual soldiers can select the comrades fitted for some especial danger, better than the commander. Hannibal employs much the same method, Livy XXI. 54.

quia quamquam &c. 'because though it was an encounter of the prepared with the unprepared, it was also an encounter of a woman with men.' It is hardly true to say that *mulier* equals *homo effeminatus* in § 84. It is rather a case of the common omission of 'like' in a simile, e.g. Hor. Ep. I. 2. 42 *qui recte vivendi prorogat annum, rusticus expectat dum defluat amnis*, i.e. 'is *like* the rustic waiting.'

§ 56. **satis fere,** 'fairly well.'

semper ille. *Ille* when indicating M. is far more emphatic than as applied to Cl., for whom it is regularly used. Trans. 'not he, he always knew' &c.

odio esse, regular passive of *odi*.

propositam...addictam. According to the commentators these words are metaphors from auctions, 'put up for sale and almost knocked down.' If so, it seems to me that *maximis praemiis*, which cannot mean 'to the highest bid,' is very awkward and inappropriate. What have rewards to do with an auction? I should prefer to take *propositam* &c. *either* (1) 'made the subject of the highest rewards,' *praemiis* being dative (cp. *vita telis fortunae proposita*, Ad Fam. v. 16. 2; *iudiciis magistratuum propositam vitam debere habemus*, Rep. IV. 12), or (2) 'posted up *with* the highest rewards (offered),' *praemiis* being abl. of attendant circumstances. Again *addictam* may be a metaphor from the process of *addictio*, by which a person became the bondsman of another. Cp. Pro Sest. § 38 *quos improbitas tribuno plebis constrictos addixerat*. Trans. 'he knew that a price had been set upon his life, and that he could hardly call it his own.'

custodia, 'precaution against surprise,' **praesidium** 'protection against attack.' A dog's bark is a *custodia*, his bite is a *praesidium*.

Martem communem, 'the impartiality of the war god.' A common expression derived from Homer Il. XVIII. 309 ξυνὸς Ἐννάλιος καί τε κτανέοντα κατέκτα (cp. Archilochus ἐτήτυμον γὰρ ξυνὸς ἀνθρώποις Ἄρης). The Latin phrase is given De Or. III. 167 as an instance of metonymy and is used several times, e.g. Ad Fam. VI. 4 *cum omnis belli Mars communis et cum semper incerti exitus proeliorum sint;* Phil. X. 20 *incertos exitus esse belli Martemque communem.* As the phrase is generally *Mars* *belli communis*, probably *pugnarum* should be taken with *Martem* as well as with *exitus*.

perculit ab abiecto, i.e. according to Halm *fecit ut ab abiecto percelleretur;* rather 'struck him down with a blow from the hand of his prostrate victim.' The *ab* may perhaps be roughly paralleled by the banking phrase *solvere ab aliquo* 'to pay through.' But probably the uniqueness of the phrase is largely due to the peculiarity of the idea. The blow appears to come from the victim, but it is really the god using him as his instrument. Purton quotes Eur. Phoenissae 1416 &c., where Eteocles while spoiling the prostrate Polynices is stabbed by him.

haesit in iis poenis, 'he was trapped,' perhaps a metaphor from liming birds, so often *aucupor*.

§ 57. **cur igitur.** Why then, asks the accuser, if the slaves were the chief actors in the tragedy did M. enfranchise them and thus prevent them from being examined by torture?

scilicet, ironical.

indicaretur, in the usual sense of evidence from an accomplice.

facti)(iuris, v. on § 15. The fallacy is obvious. Putting aside the fact (apparently true, but persistently ignored by C.) that Cl. was not killed in a scuffle, but in cold blood afterwards, the slaves could obviously state *uter insidiator esset*.

C. XXII. **nescis inimici factum**, 'you don't understand the art of attacking your enemy,' i.e. you might more plausibly accuse him of having been ungenerous to his slaves, because he *only* enfranchised them.

§ 58. **placata est**, so the riot is calmed by the *vir pietate gravis* in Aen. I. 151 &c.

propter quos, *propter = per*, a usage found, in Cicero at any rate, only of *persons*, cp. § 81. It seems to be (mainly at any rate) confined to cases where a contrast is drawn between what we owe to a person, and the way it is requited to him. So Rosc. Am. 13 *privare luce eos propter quos lucem aspexerat;* Piso 15 *incendere domum eius propter quem urbs incensa non est;* Ad Fam. VII. 24. 4 *me propter quem ceteri liberi sunt, tibi liberum non visum.* The same contrast appears though not so strongly marked in § 93 *re publica sine me sed propter me perfruantur,* and in *propter eosdem* below. It is a natural consequence of this, that it is usually found with a relative; but Dräger, Hist. Syn. § 258, is obviously wrong in saying that C. only uses it with relatives.

quam quod, 'as the fact that.'

dedendi fuerunt, v. on *optabilius,* § 31.

quod minus moleste ferat, litotes for 'which gives him so much comfort.'

si quid accidat, euphemistic for 'if he is condemned' (elsewhere as in § 99 = 'die'). So *calamitas* and συμφορὰ in Greek; 'unfortunate' in certain circles in England has much the same meaning.

§ 59. **sed** not *at.* The fact that the torture of Cl.'s slaves is (though unjustly) telling against (*urgent*) Milo, is admitted by C., not quoted as an adversary's objection. This seems to me better than to say that *sed* is simply resumptive or transitional.

nunc, 'lately.' Cp. *centum dies* § 60.

Appius. Nephew of Clodius, v. Intr. p. xxii.

unde? ab Appio, 'from what house? from that of Appius.' The injustice apparently consists in two points, (1) the prosecutor was not allowed to offer his own slaves for examination by torture, (2) they ought to have been put into confinement directly there was any idea of examining them (*conici in arcas* § 60), not produced straight from the house with every opportunity of priming them. As to no. (1) Eberhard quotes Dig. 48. 18. 1 § 3 *ad quaestionem non esse provocandos eos, quos accusator de domo sua produxit.* A special concession appears to have been made to Appius by Domitius in consideration of M. having manumitted *his* slaves (Asc. § 25).

quid potest agi severius? 'could any proceeding be more strictly just?' (ironical). So *certius, integrius, incorruptius,* below. Beware of translating 'harsh.'

de servis &c. The connection of thought must be carefully observed. 'The evidence of Cl.'s slaves tells against M. very likely, but what is it worth? It was bad enough to demand (as the Appii did) to have M.'s slaves examined. Such a demand was unprecedented, and absurdly out of proportion to the importance of the case. Still I do admit in such a case that the truth might be discovered. But when the accuser's slaves are tortured under such conditions as Cl.'s have been, there is no chance of getting the truth.'

nulla, perhaps agreeing with *quaestio.* Cp. Phil. ii. 56 *nullum fuisse de alea lege iudicium.* But *legibus* would be more usual than *lege,* and it makes perhaps better sense to take *nulla* as ablative. None of the various laws regulating justice (with one exception) enforced *quaestio in dominum* (and therefore the owner could always refuse to produce his slaves). For the special exception made with regard to *incestum* cp. Partit. Orat. § 118 where we find that a similar exception was also made in the case of the Catilinarian conspirators. Cp. also Pro Deiot. § 3, and App. I. in Mr Poynton's edition.

deos, governed by *proxime* not *accessit*, R. 1106 c. The same construction perhaps occurs in Acad. II. 36, where see Reid's note.

ipsos, i.e. *ad bonam deam.*

sed tamen, often used to mark a resumption after a parenthesis like 'well' or 'I say,' Zumpt 739. Here however the '*tamen*' may be more forcible, 'still I admit that our ancestors' objection was a sentimental one, not founded on the worthlessness of the evidence thus extracted.'

non quin, 'not because not,' followed like *non quod* by a subjunctive, R. 1744.

§ 60. **heus...sis** (=*si vis*), colloquial. **verbi causa**, 'to take any name at random.'

Rufio, 'Ginger.' 'The ancient slave was represented on the stage as red haired,' Tyrrell on Att. v. 2.

sperata libertas, put instead of *spes libertatis* to balance *certa crux.*

subito abrepti tamen, 'even when carried off without notice for torture, slaves are isolated and thrown into cages,' i.e. the fact that slaves' evidence is liable to be tampered with is so fully recognized by the law, that *even* when arrest is unexpected, further precautions are taken. How absurd then to rely on the examination of slaves who have been under the control of the prosecutor without any restriction.

arcas, 'cells,' root *arc* 'to confine.'

ab eo ipso accusatore, *ab* perhaps 'from the house,' as *ab Appio* above. But it may equally well be ablative of *agent* corresponding to *quis produxit?* The fact that Appius had every opportunity of tampering with them is sufficiently emphasised by *centum dies penes accusatorem.*

C. XXIII. § 61. **res ipsa**, 'the story of the deed itself,' i.e. the circumstances attending the murder itself as opposed to Milo's behaviour after it. We now turn from the *res*, and discuss the *post rem.* Elsewhere as in § 66 *res ipsa* simply means 'the facts.'

exanimatum, 'paralysed,' opposite of *praesentiam animi.*

neque vero &c., i.e. he put himself (1) in the hands of the people, (2) the senate, (3) the regular executive, (4) the special powers of Pompey.

omnem pubem Italiae commiserat, i.e. given powers to levy troops throughout Italy.

magna vis conscientiae.   Cp. Cat. III. 27 *magna vis consci-entiae quam qui negligent cum me violare volent, se indicabunt.* Id. 11, *quanta vis esset conscientiae.* In cases like these the word is equivalent to our 'conscience' except that it does not include 'the power of conscience to restrain' (*religio*) or the faculty of moral judgment; v. Nettleship 'Contributions to Lat. Lexicography.'

§ 62.   **ratione certa,** 'rational grounds,' opposed (Pro Man. § 43) to *opinio et fama.* So in next line *ratio facti* 'reasonable-ness.'

constantia defensionis, either 'the consistency of his de-fence,' i.e. a defence in which *omnia constabant,* or better, 'the courage and firmness he shewed in defending himself.'

imperitorum, 'who did not know M.'s character.' Halm. But *imperitus* is a standing epithet with C. to express the weak-headedness of the public, well disposed in themselves, but incapable of rising above *opinio et sermones,* and a prey to agitators. So e.g. Clu. § 5 *invidia valeat in opinionibus ac sermonibus imperitorum, ab ingeniis prudentium repudietur.* So frequently with *multitudo,* cp. § 90.   Livy XLV. 23 *nulla enim est civitas, quae non et improbos cives aliquando et impe-ritam multitudinem semper habeat.* Our own 'ignorant' has much the same shade of meaning.

§ 63.   **illud,** explained by the substantival clause *ut...ini-micum.* We may translate 'whether he had done the deed in passion and excitement, *and* filled with hatred murdered his enemy.' The addition of the *illud* marks this off, I think, from the *periphrasis* with *facere ut* noticed in § 95. So Verr. Act. I. 55 *faciam hoc non novum...ut testibus utar statim;* Lucr. III. 911 *hoc etiam faciunt...homines...ut dicant.*

patria ut careret, v. on *vindicaret,* § 38. Here however the *oratio recta* might be *putavit tanti ut careat,* 'he thought it of such value, that he *will* give up.'

non dubitaturum...quin, 'he would not hesitate to bow contentedly to the law.' But the infinitive after *dubito* in this sense, is more usual. Cp. *dubitarit aperire,* § 44, Madv. § 375.

haec, i.e. Rome (as representing the Roman Empire). The phrase is frequently used with *servare, stare* and their opposites *delere, perire.* Cp. Cat. I. 21, IV. 7; Sulla 32. 76. Other in-stances are given by Näg. § 50.

fruenda. For the gerundive used as though *fruor* was transitive, v. R. pref. LXXVII. The usage is probably due to the fact that *fruor was* originally transitive.

illa portenta, 'these monstrosities,' i.e. the Catilinarians. Sometimes the phrase is *portentum reipublicae.*

loquebantur, 'prated of,' = *usurpo*, v. instances in L. and S.

erumpet, cp. the famous *abiit, excessit, evasit, erupit*, of Catiline ii. 1.

miseros interdum. 'How unhappy sometimes is the lot of the best patriot.'

§ 64. **ergo**, 'so then,' perhaps either strictly causal, 'so then since he did return, you see that these suspicions were false,' or 'well then,' resumptive after the digression *multi etiam...suspicantur. Illa* can only refer to the report that he had gone into honourable exile. C. would never admit that M. under any circumstances could imitate Catiline.

C. xxiv. **quemvis...conscientia**, 'any one *with* a consciousness of even comparatively venial misdeeds.' *conscientia* abl. of description. Cp. De Am. 54 *quamquam miror illa superbia, et importunitate, si quemquam amicum habere potuit.* Others take it as a sort of causal abl. with *perculissent.*

frenorum. The word has been a stumbling block to many editors. But there is no reason why M. should not have been credited with intending to equip a troop of horse. What difficulty there is, is largely removed by the arrangement of words in Nohl's edition *pilorum frenorum etiam*, 'swords, shields, pila and even bridles.' The accumulation of words in *orum* does not seem to have offended the Roman ear. Cp. Rosc. Am. § 103, Cat. i. 7, where other instances are quoted by Wilkins.

indicabatur, v. note on *liberatur*, § 47. The same usage is found in Cicero with *audior* and *scribor.*

Miloni, dat. of advantage.

devecta Tiberi, i.e. from the uplands: Ocriculum is above Rome.

domus referta, a relapse from the construction of *dicebant* to that of *indicabatur.*

malleolorum. Cp. Cat. i. 32 *malleolos et faces ad inflammandam urbem comparare.* The *malleolus* was 'a reed shaft, fitted at the top with a frame of wire work, like the head of a distaff, which was filled with inflammable materials such as tow steeped in pitch, and had an arrow head affixed to the top, so that the whole figure resembled a mallet. It was set alight before being discharged, and when it reached the object against which it was directed, the arrow head stuck firmly into it while the tow blazed away, and ignited whatever it had fastened upon.' Rich.

incendia, i.e. in different places. The conspirator *discripsit urbis partes ad incendia*, Cat. i. 9.

delata, i.e., to Pompey.

quaesita sunt, 'investigated,' a rare use for *de iis quaesitum est.* Cp. Pro Caec. 97 *re quaesita et deliberata.*

§ 65.   **popa,** 'the slaughterer.' The *popa* was an assistant of the priest who killed the victim with a mallet or axe.   Cp. Persius 6. 74 *popa venter,* generally supposed to refer to the corpulence of the *popa* 'a belly as fat as that of a *popa.*' [But why not a belly as big as a *popa?*   A slaughterer is naturally big, not necessarily fat.]   From Asconius it appears that this Licinius was a *sacrificulus qui solitus erat familias purgare,* i.e. an inferior priest who offered sacrifices for slaves.   Such a *sacrificulus* would probably be his own *popa,* and Cicero to discredit his evidence gives him the more menial name.

servos Milonis, sc. *cum diceret,* so Livy iv. 20 *quum Augustum se ipsum scriptum legisse audissem,* 'I heard Augustus say that he had read.'

apud se, i.e., according to editors, in a *popina* or restaurant where the *popa* sold the remains of the victim. [I do not know on what authority this rests, except that Nettleship, 'Contributions to Latin Lexicography,' quotes *popa = tabernarius* from the 'Epinal glossary.'   There seems no reason to connect *popa* philologically with *popina,* which is probably from the root of *coquo* labialised.]   Otherwise 'at his own house,' where the slaves had come to be purified.

coniurasse, for the omission of *se* v. note on *exiturum,* § 52.

in hortos, so Asc. intr. § 16 *plerumque non domi suae, sed in hortis manebat, idque ipsum in superioribus, circa quos magna manus militum excubabat.*

de amicorum sententia, cp. the common phrase *de consilii sententia,* which always accompanied the decrees of provincial governors.   'At Rome, custom in all cases, and law in many cases required that decisions on all important matters should not be taken by public officers, or even *patres-familiarum,* without consultation with those best qualified to advise them.' Reid.

confessionem servorum.   Edd. quote Paul. Dig. 48, 18, 18 *servo qui ultro aliquid de domino confitetur, fides non accommodatur,* cp. § 59.

probari pro, 'pass for,' 'be regarded as.'   So *falsa pro veris probare,* Acad. ii. 66 &c.

§ 66.   **ne vos aliquid timeretis,** *aliquid* for *quid* to emphasise the antithesis to *omnia.*   Zumpt 708, Madv. 493.

audierat, 'had (actually) heard,' *audiebatur* 'received a hearing.'

celebri loco, i.e. in the *via sacra.* Caesar as *pontifex maximus* had official quarters at the *Regia,* v. § 37.

re publica suscepta, i.e. by being sole consul; or more generally as being the pillar of the state, cp. § 19.

senator, his name was Cornificius, Asc. §17.

cum telo, cp. § 11.

in sanctissimo templo. The senate could only be held in a *templum* i.e. *in loco per augurem constituto.* For *nudavit* Halm quotes Valerius Maximus 2. 47 *in aliquo sacrato loco nudare se nefas esse credebatur.*

ut eo tacente, 'so that the facts spoke for themselves without a word from him.' It should be carefully observed that *ut loqueretur* is consecutive, otherwise *se* not *eo* would be used. R. 2267.

C. xxv. § 67. **omnia...timemus.** A difficult passage which has been emended in various ways. The MS. reading labours under two objections, (1) that though *cum tamen*= 'and yet at the same time,' has authority in Cicero and elsewhere, it is quite out of place at the beginning of a conditional sentence, (2) what is the sense of *si metuitur Milo, timemus* &c.? It must mean I suppose, 'If M. is feared by the jury (and therefore we have to fear that the jury will condemn him) they fear him not because he murdered Cl., but because they think Pompey's suspicions are probably just.' This is very strained (*subinepti aliquid habet haec timoris longe diversi in protasi et apodosi coniunctio,* Madvig). Both objections are removed by the simple omission of *si.* The sentence then runs *omnia falsa atque insidiose ficta comperta sunt: cum tamen metuitur etiam nunc Milo. Non iam hoc* &c. 'All these statements are proved to be lies, and yet Pompey continues to fear Milo. It is not now the charge of the murder that Milo has to fear, but Pompey's suspicions.' Amongst the emendations may be noticed *quod si metuitur; verum tamen si metuitur; cum tamen si metuitur Miloni* (which removes the second but not the first objection). For *cum tamen* in this sense with the indicative, cp. Piso § 27, Verres 5, § 74, and several instances in Lucretius (v. Munro on i. 566).

crimen Clodianum, 'the charge of murdering Cl.,' cp. *crimen Asuvianum,* Pro Clu. § 39. Such adjectives are formed in Latin far more easily than in English. 'Puseyite,' even 'Gladstonian' and 'Peelite' have a touch of slang about them.

te enim appello, Pompey was seated in front of the Treasury, at some distance from Cicero.

exaudire, 'to catch what I say.' The question is often

raised whether *exaudio* means 'to hear distinctly,' or 'to hear in spite of some obstacle such as distance, or weakness of voice,' compare e.g. Holden on Planc. § 97, with Reid on Sulla § 33. The present passage illustrates how closely the two meanings are allied. Ordinary hearing *is* 'distinct hearing,' but we only call it so when some obstacle has been overcome. 'I heard you quite distinctly,' does not imply that we heard better than ordinarily, but that for some reason or other, we might have expected not to hear.

aliquando aliquid, cf. Sest. 14 *si qui aliquid aliquando fecerunt.* Ac. II. 25 *si aliquid aliquando acturus est.* 'The common supposition that words with *ali-* used with *si* are stronger than the simple forms is not always borne out by the passages.' Reid on De Am. 24.

conquisitores, 'recruiting officers,' in earlier times mainly employed at great emergencies. After B.C. 89 when all Italy became liable to service it was usual to employ them.

si excubiae, si vigiliae, when C. uses *excubiae* he seems always to couple it with either *vigiliae* or *custodiae.* So too *excubabo et vigilabo pro vobis,* Phil. VI. 18. Cp. our own phrase 'watch and ward.' There does not seem any clearly marked distinction between the words.

non unius viri, 'more than that of a mere individual.'

§ 68. **aegras** corresponds to *sanares, labantes* to *confirmares.*

locus, 'opportunity.' Pompey had refused to see Milo.

neminem umquam &c. 'that no one ever loved his fellow man better than he loved you.' Cicero regularly uses *nemo homo* not *nullus homo,* so with other nouns denoting persons. Cp. Zumpt § 676.

postea defensum, cp. § 40.

petitione praeturae, M. was praetor in 55.

sperasse se habere, 'trusted that he had,' *sperasse se habiturum* 'he hoped to have.'

te tuo beneficio. Tacitus says that *odisse quem laeseris* is natural. Cicero here implies that *amare cui benefeceris* is equally so.

probaret...inhaesisset...cessisset...antestaretur, observe the mixture of tenses. This irregularity is sometimes found in C., e.g. De Am. 13 *quod non fecissent (maiores) si nihil ad eos pertinere arbitrarentur,* on which v. Dr Reid who regards it as an irregularity of the same nature as the historic present, i.e. used for vividness. The explanation that the imperfect repre-

sents the action as 'accompanying and continuing along with
the action of the principal verb' (Madv. §347) may suit *non
probaret*, but hardly *antestaretur*.

ne 'assuredly.' Always used with personal and demonstra-
tive pronouns (and generally in a conditional sentence), v.
L. and S. For *iste* used of the client instead of the opponent
in a lawsuit cp. Clu. 201, Planc. 99.

is qui ita natus est et ita consuevit = *cuius talis est natura,
et consuetudo*, cp. §36. For the pleonastic *is*, cp. *eam* §95.

antestaretur, 'he would call you to witness his protest.'
If the defendant in a suit refused to follow the plaintiff into
court, the latter might use force, *having first called on a
bystander to bear witness* (if required) *that he had summoned
him properly*. This is called *antestatio*: v. examples in L. and
S. So here Milo would solemnly protest his fidelity to Pompey
and his country and call P. to witness that he had done so.
The difficulty of the word is, I think, exaggerated by many
editors. It is true that Milo is not a plaintiff summoning a
defendant: but otherwise he does exactly what was done in
antestatio, he makes a protest, calls upon someone else to hear
it and to bear witness to it, when required at some future
time. The correction *ante testaretur* is easy, and has fair
MS. authority, but I cannot think it is, as Mr Clark says,
'certain' or approaching certainty.

quod nunc etiam facit, i.e. 'as you would not listen to his
protest at a private interview, he makes it now.' Halm takes
nunc etiam to mean 'even now while he still hopes to convince
you.'

C. XXVI. §69.   **vides,** for the alliteration v. on §30.

ratio vitae, 'the course of life,' so *ratio comitiorum* Mur. 35,
ratio tempestatum id. 4.

infidelitates, '*instances* of infidelity.' The whole sentence
well illustrates this Latin use of the plural of abstract substantives.

ad tempus aptae, 'time serving.'

erit, erit profecto, the time will come when you will be
reminded of Milo's protest, just as the witness is reminded of
the *antestatio*.

salutaribus, almost = *salvis*. No other instance is quoted,
but the word is not so strained, as if applied to a person. So
in English we can say 'disastrous position,' but not 'disastrous
person.'

motu communium temporum, 'in some revolution of public
affairs.' Cp. Balb. §58 *ut in me unum incumberet omnis illa*

inclinatio communium temporum, where *inclinatio = motus* here and *communia* = 'national' as opposed to *privata*. The abl. abs. *motu aliquo* is harsh. Some MSS. have *in* after *aliquo*, perhaps a corruption of *immutatis* or *inclinatis* or *impendente*.

qui quam crebro, 'and how frequently that happens, experience should have taught us.'

unius...fortissimi. 'The man of all men unmatched in bravery, since the birth of mankind.' For this use of *unus* emphasising superlatives and kindred words, v. Mayor on Phil. II. 84, Madv. 310, Zumpt 691.

desideres, subj. because it depends on *dies cum = dies talis ut in eo*, v. Madv. § 358, obs. 4, Zumpt 579.

§ 70.   quamquam, cp. § 6.

iuris publici &c. The three elements of a statesman's knowledge—constitutional law, historical precedent and political experience (*res publica*).

ne quid detrimenti &c. This is the famous *senatus consultum ultimum*, by which, since the practical disuse of the dictatorship, the senate claimed the right to invest the magistrates in emergencies with dictatorial powers, and thus 'relieve them of responsibility for any illegal act that they might be driven to commit in the rapid execution of their duty,' Heitland on Pro Rabirio App. A, where an excellent discussion of the whole subject will be found.

versiculo, 'line.' The associations of the word 'verse' with poetry, make us apt to forget that *versus* in Latin is equally applicable to a line of prose.

nullis armis datis, this is not strictly true, as one of the powers which the *ultimum decretum* tacitly gave the consuls was *parare exercitum*, Sallust Cat. 29. But on this occasion it was *expressly* decreed *ut dilectum Pompeius tota Italia haberet*.

qui tolleret, 'who as you say was subverting.'

oporteret...liceret, consecutive subjunctive. For the tense cp. *adepti estis ne metueretis* § 34, *iudicaretis* § 11 with note.

§ 71.   in illo loco, i.e. where he can command the forum, cp. on § 67.

posset, 'would be able,' sc. *si vellet*. So Eberhard. Rather 'might have punished.' The subj. is sufficiently accounted for by its dependence on the infinitive *cogere*. R. 1776.

more maiorum. 'There was no *lex* in grant or confirmation of the right of the senate to issue the *ultimum decretum*.

Where we find any reference to its basis, it is in effect made to rest on custom and usage only. The very anxiety of Cicero to give it the appearance of immemorial antiquity arises from a consciousness of the lack of other authority.' Heitland, Pro Rab. App. A.

suo iure, 'under his own jurisdiction' (without calling in the aid of the law courts).

contra hesternam illam contionem, cp. § 3.

C. XXVII. § 72. **nec vero me.** Connect as Halm with *quid sentiatis libere iudicare.* The sense is 'if Pompey wishes you to vote according to your feelings, I can have no doubt about those feelings. I am not afraid of the *crimen Clodianum,* in fact I know that M.'s killing him is a merit in your eyes.'

expers = *ignarus*: so *expers iuris,* 'ignorant of law,' Leg. I. 14, Livy IX. 9. The usage does not appear to be common: *consilii expers,* 'excluded from the plan,' which is quoted by Eberhard, is somewhat different.

si iam, 'supposing for the moment,' v. Munro on Lucr. I. 968, Madv. De Fin. IV. 66.

diluere crimen. Grk. διαλύειν τὴν διαβολήν.

mentiri gloriose, 'the falsehood would but bring him glory,' *gloriose* in the sense of 'gloriously' not 'boastfully.' Cp. Eur. Bacchae 334 καταψεύδου καλῶς, and the famous *splendide mendax* of Hor. Odes III. 11. 35. [There however the thought is somewhat different: the motive of the lie, not as here the substance of it, is glorious.] The phrase 'to glory in the lie,' which Purton and Poynton give, seems to me too stamped with an unfavourable sense to be an adequate translation here.

iacturis, 'sacrifices.'

collegae, i.e. the tribune Octavius, who vetoed the agrarian law of Gracchus and was deposed by vote of the people.

per seditionem, 'unconstitutionally,' Eberhard. Rather 'by seditious means.' The *seditiosus* excites the passions of the populace, cp. *seditiose* § 8. Compare Juv. II. 24 *quis tulerit Gracchos de seditione querentes?*

conprehenderunt, 'detected,' more often *deprehenderunt,* but cp. Cat. III. 3 *investigata et comprehensa.* Pro Cael. 64 *ut facinus comprehenderetur,* &c.

§ 73. **eum cuius** &c., 'whose punishment the senate frequently declared to be necessary to cleanse the sacred rites from pollution.' *Religiones expiare* like *locum* or *ea quae violata sunt expiare.*

sorore, i.e. Clodius' younger sister, Lucullus' wife.

iuratus, i.e. at the trial of Cl. for sacrilege.

quaestionibus habitis, to be taken with *comperisse* not *dixit.* The order of events was (1) Lucullus held a private investigation (*quaestiones*), where the slaves were tortured in the presence of a family council: cp. Pro Clu. 176, (2) he divorced his wife, (3) afterwards when Cl. was on his trial he gave (in evidence) the history of this investigation.

eum, qui civem, *civis* here is Cicero: a few lines below, Pompey.

regna dedit, i.e. to Brogitarus of Galatia, on whom the title of king was conferred by a law proposed by Clodius B.C. 58. This was regarded as an encroachment on the rights of the senate.

ademit, i.e. from Ptolemy of Cyprus, in the same year: for these laws v. Pro Sest. §§ 56, 57.

quibuscum voluit &c., i.e. brought in a law assigning Macedonia and Cilicia to the consuls Gabinius and Piso in defiance of the *Lex Sempronia,* by which the senate before the election of consuls determined to what provinces they should go after their year of office. Cp. Pro Sest. § 53.

cui nihil umquam &c., 'who regarded no evil deed or thought as sinful.'

qui aedem Nympharum incendit. In Pro Cael. 78 the fire is ascribed to Sextus Clodius.

ut memoriam publicam &c., i.e. to confuse voters and non-voters. So Oppianicus *corrupit publicas censorias tabulas* at Larinum. Pro Clu. § 41.

publicam...publicis, 'national.' The word enhances the wickedness of the act.

§ 74. **denique.** With this word C. passes from Cl.'s public to his private crimes.

cui iam &c., 'who had ceased to regard statute, law or landmark.'

ius civile, 'the law of the land,' i.e. the rules and principles which govern the relation of Roman citizens, derived partly from *leges* or written enactment, partly from other sources (**v.** Nettleship, 'Contributions' on *ius* and *lex*).

calumnia litium=*calumniosis litibus,* 'dishonest and vexatious lawsuits.' *Calumniari est falsa crimina intendere,* Marcianus Dig. 48, 16, 1. '*Calumnia* signifies the taking of legal proceedings when one has good reason for believing that the charge has no foundation.' Dict. of Ant.

vindiciis ac sacramentis. In a dispute as to property, the persons, who claimed it, first made a formal claim (*vindicatio* or *vindiciae*) before the praetor, and then deposited a sum of money to be forfeited by the loser. This sum was called *sacramentum* perhaps because deposited in an *aedes sacra*. The name is frequently transferred to the *claim* or challenge of which the deposit was the token. Thus here and often elsewhere we find *iustum* or *iniustum sacramentum*. The word is fully illustrated in L. and S.

signis inferendis, i.e. with regular military assaults : take *inferendis* with *signis* only.

Etruscos, cp. §§ 26, 50, 55.

contempserat. Obs. the pluperfect combined with the imperfects. *Feeling* precedes *action*, and therefore the verb which expresses the former is regarded as belonging to an earlier time than those which express the latter. So in § 43. Cp. Livy II. 50 *Iamque adeo contempserant Fabii hostem ut...crederent:* cp. also *terminarat* below, *concupierat* in § 52.

hunc iudicem nostrum, cp. § 16.

Ianiculo, i.e. the northern bank of the Tiber.

splendido, 'magnificent,' a standing epithet of the *equites*. Grk. μεγαλοπρεπής: one who does things on a large scale—a natural epithet for a class of capitalists.

arma, either 'tools' or 'weapons.' The former seems to be approved by most editors, but there is a great absence of authority for any such meaning. Such phrases as *cerealia arma* Aen. I. 177, *quae sint duris agrestibus arma* Georg. I. 160, *arma apta tondendis capillis* Mart. XIV. 36, or even Caesar B. G. III. 14 *naves armorum omni genere ornatissimae*, are very meagre evidence. On the other hand, if the word means 'arms,' its conjunction with *materiem* &c. is a παρὰ προσδοκίαν savouring more of modern rhetoricians than of Cicero, though the objection that Cl.'s men would *bear* arms themselves and not need to have them conveyed is not very weighty. Cicero may well have overlooked so minor an inconsistency, in order to draw a vivid picture. A possible solution of the difficulty is to read with the Cologne MS. *harenam*, 'sand' (mixed with *calx* 'lime' to make mortar). V. Clark p. XLVII.

trans ripam, 'from the other bank.' 'The bank' is regarded as being strictly the edge of the land, not the land near the edge. So we might say 'he fell *over* the bank.' Cp. Ovid Met. IX. 114 *curvos trans ripam miserat arcus.*

§ 75. **cui viro**, 'a man like him!' in contrast to *muliercula* and *adulescens*. I doubt whether this is said (as Eberhard) in 'bitter scorn.' We should not think it so bad to attack a man, as a woman. Cicero does not share this chivalrous idea. The fact that Cl. attacked Furfanius is a proof of his *audacia*.

sed, resumptive after the parenthesis: v. on *sed tamen* § 59, Madv. 480.

ausum esse, governed by *dico* understood out of *quid dicam.*

quantam poposcerat, 'the amount, whatever it was, that he asked.' The indicative shews that it is *not* the *oratio obliqua* of *nisi, quantum poposci, dederis.* Cl. asked a stated sum.

mortuum, here used as a substantive, a use generally confined to the plural. Cp. *effigies spirantis mortui,* Ad Quint. I. 3, 1. Näg. § 28.

qua invidia *&c.* = *cuius rei invidia &c.*—'the odium of which, he thought (or 'said'), must blast the character of such a man.'

conflagrandum, v. on *ambustus* § 12. Cp. Cat. I. 29 *tum te non intelligis invidiae incendio conflagraturum.*

huic tali viro. The words, as it seems to me, emphasise the absurdity of Cl.'s threat: he actually pretended that so absurd a charge could annihilate a man of Furfanius' character. The *audacia* then consists in his trying to extort money, with no stronger weapon than this. If this explanation is wrong, the words must bring out the wickedness of Cl.'s thought; he wished to blast the character of a particularly excellent man.

mihi. This of course is Cicero, though Milo is supposed to be speaking throughout this section. Even in reporting real conversations, it is not unusual for the reporter to drift away into his own thoughts. Cp. Epistle to the Galatians ii. 14 and Lightfoot's note. It is still more natural in an imaginary conversation.

absentem deiecit. *Deicere* is the technical term for forcible occupation of another man's property. Cp. Pro Caec. § 34 &c. where C. argues that anyone who *vi prohibet* may be said *deicere.*

vestibulum, 'fore-court,' defined by Aulus Gellius 16, 5 as *locus ante ianuam domus vacuus per quem a via aditus accessusque ad aedes est, cum dextra sinistraque tecta sunt,* i.e. a court surrounded on three sides and open on the fourth to the road.

aditus, 'entrance from the road': *limen,* entrance into the house. The same words are somewhat differently combined Pro Caec. 35 *si non modo limine tectoque aedium, sed primo aditu vestibuloque prohibuissent.*

C. XXVIII. § 76. **nescio quo modo,** not 'imperceptibly' as

Mr Poynton. Rather perhaps 'unfortunately.' The phrase is generally used of something unavoidable, but to be regretted. Cp. e.g. Acad. II. 9 *nescio quomodo plerique errare malunt*, v. Holden on De Off. I. 146.

imperium, i.e. the praetorship.

si nactus esset. There is no formal apodosis to this, but it is easily supplied out of the words that follow, 'he would have attacked not only foreign princes, but you, your property, and your families.'

tetrarchas, generally coupled with *reges*, v. Merivale on Sall. Cat. 20.

pecunias, 'property.' Halm says 'moveable property,' but the word need not be so limited. Cp. Rosc. Am. § 6, where the context shews that land is included. *Pecuniam dicit universitatem rei familiaris*, Schol.

tenentur, 'are ascertained facts,' cp. Att. XIV. 9 *Iam tenetur venisse cum maximis copiis Pacorum Parthum*.

§ 77. tenens gladium, short for *prae se tenens*, as of L. Brutus after Lucretia's death, Liv. I. 59. Cp. Phil. II. 30.

cervicibus, C. does not use *cervix* in the singular. The metaphor seems to be sometimes from a yoke or burden, as in *legiones in cervicibus collocare*, Ad Fam. XII. 23, sometimes from beheading, as Phil. II. 51 *cervices subiecit securi*.

ius, aequitas. *Ius* is the actual embodiment of justice—law, and law-courts—*aequitas* the quality of justice. *Ius* (if misused) may cease to be justice, not so *aequitas*. Naturally the distinction often rises to an opposition (as between our own 'law' and 'equity'), e.g. Phil. IX. 11.

pudor, pudicitia, 'modesty, chastity,' *pudor animi, pudicitia corporis*, Manutius (quoted by Fausset on Pro Clu. § 12).

vero, v. on *id vero* § 53.

unum...plurimum profuisse, v. on § 69.

non queo. Cicero does not use *nequeo* in the 1st person [except in the metrical translation of Aeschylus, Tusc. II. 24].

multas victorias, e.g. Marius over the Cimbri and Teutones, Crassus over Spartacus, Pompey over Mithridates.

§ 78. hoc, i.e. what follows; namely that your prosperity would have been impossible but for Cl.'s death.

ita existimabitis, 'you will have this thought,' the clause following explains *ita*. The construction is more common with *sic*, e.g. Pro Man. § 47.

spem verissimam, 'well-grounded,' so *verus timor*, Cat. I. 18.

constitutis, opp. to *tollo* § 70.

privata, opp. to *in republica bona*.

quod ius perpetuae &c., 'what guarantee of lasting tenure would have belonged to them.' *Ius* here is 'a right which can practically be enforced,' almost = 'power' as in the phrase *sui iuris esse*. For the whole phrase cp. Pro Flacco § 80 *habeant ius civile praedia*.

C. XXIX.   **odio inimicitiarum**, 'hatred arising from personal enmity,' gen. of possession: the plural is the regular form, the singular being apparently only used in good prose as an abstract philosophical term, v. Heitland on Mur. § 56, where the same phrase occurs.

libentius quam verius, 'with more zest than justice.' Obs. the well-known idiom of the double comparative, Madv. 307, Zumpt 690.

praecipuum, 'superlative as my hatred was bound to be.'

ut in communi odio, 'that it hardly outstepped the limits of the general hate.'

§ 79.   **quin sic attendite** &c., 'rather look at the matter in the following light: this is obviously an enquiry into the death of Clodius.' He goes on to say that they would not have Cl. alive, if they could : how absurd then that they should be engaged on such an enquiry!

cogitationes, 'the imagination,' cp. Balb. § 47 *existat ergo ille vir parumper cogitatione vestra, quoniam re non potest, ut conspiciatis eum mentibus quem iam oculis non potestis.*

ut ea cernimus, quae videmus, 'as we discern the objects which meet our bodily eye,' *video* being confined to the mere impression upon the retina. The Cologne MS. has *ut ea cernamus quae non videmus*, a thought which is thoroughly Ciceronian, cp. Balb. 47 quoted above, Or. 18 *cernebat animo, re ipsa non videbat*, and an unidentified passage quoted by Quint. IX. 2, 41 *haec quae non vidistis oculis, animis cernere potestis*. Both readings, though especially the first, seem to me to labour under the difficulty that they suppose a distinction between *cerno* and *video*, which cannot be made out. The evidence tends to shew that while C. is very fond of using both verbs in the same passage, he uses them very indiscriminately (v. exx. quoted by Reid on Ac. II. 80, to which may be added Tusc. I. 56, 67, De Div. I. 126, De Sen. 83, De Fin. III. 48). Thus while in the two passages quoted above we have *cerno* of intellectual perception, *video* of bodily, explanatory

words such as *animis, oculis*, are added; and in Ad Fam. vi. 3, 2
we have *ego tam video animo, quam ea quae cernimus oculis*.
So De Or. iii. 161 *ponunt in conspectu animi, quae cernere et
videre non possumus*. I am somewhat surprised that in our
passage the conjecture of Schuetz *ut ea quae cernimus et
videmus*, which is exactly paralleled by this last quotation,
should never have found favour with editors.

fingite igitur, 'suppose then that I present you with these
alternatives,' *igitur* resumptive after the parenthesis, as *sed* in
§ 59: v. Zumpt 739.

si possim &c., 'suppose I could get you to acquit M., but
on condition that Cl. comes to life again.'

ita, si, 'on condition that.' Variations of the phrase are
ita demum si, ita tamen si, atque ita si. Cp. Pro Caec. 82
*neque enim praetor, si ex eo fundo essem deiectus, ita me restitui
iussit*. *Revixerit* is perf. subj.

quid vultu extimuistis? 'what means this look of fear?'—
an *aposiopesis* for 'would you accept the proposals?'

aut quaestionem ferre aut, 'To choose between moving
this trial and recalling Cl.' The alternatives at first sight
seem hardly to be alternatives; but throughout this section C.
admits, what is no doubt true, that the Jury and Pompey both
acted as Cl.'s *avengers* (cp. *eius sedetis ultores*). It is assumed
that the Jury meant to condemn and that Pompey meant him
to be condemned. Cicero asks them what they would do if
asked to restore the victim to life, instead of avenging him.
If they did not prefer to revive him, then their wish to avenge
him was unreasonable. The second pair of alternatives, if
expressed in the form of the first, would run *ita non ferre
quaestionem, si revixerit*. Similarly the first pair, if expressed
as the second, would be *aut condemnare Milonem aut excitare
Cl*. &c.

eadem lege. There is a confusion of language here. C.
means that if the *lex quaestionis*, instead of being a *lex quaestionis* had been a law to restore Cl. to life, it would never have
been passed. But then it obviously would not have been 'the
same law.'

ab iisne, the late position of the *ne* may be defended by
regarding *in confitendo* as a clause by itself = *si confiteretur*.
Ab iisne is regular for *abne iis*.

§ 80. **quae Athenis** &c., i.e. to Harmodius and Aristogeiton,
the murderers of Hipparchus. Cp. Dem. de Falsa Legatione
280 (321) Ἁρμοδίου καὶ Ἀριστογείτόνος...οὓς νόμῳ διὰ τὰς εὐεργε-
σίας, ἃς ὑπῆρξαν εἰς ὑμᾶς, ἐν ἅπασι τοῖς ἱεροῖς ἐπὶ ταῖς θυσίαις

σπονδῶν καὶ κρατήρων κοινωνοὺς πεποίησθε καὶ ᾄδετε καὶ τιμᾶτε ἐξ ἴσου τοῖς ἥρωσι καὶ τοῖς θεοῖς.

in aliis urbibus, e.g. probably at Corinth to Timoleon, Sicyon to the murderers of Euphron : v. Grote, Vol. III. p. 26.

quos cantus, quae carmina, e.g. the famous drinking song, 'I'll wreath my sword in a myrtle bough.' For the distinction between *carmina* and *cantus* v. L. and S. on *cantus.*

ad immortalitatis religionem, 'the sanctity that belongs to immortality,' i.e. immortals. Cp. Phil. I. 13 *mortuum cum religione immortalium coniungere.* With *memoriam* the genitive is perhaps different, 'memory equivalent to immortality,' op. Phil. II. 33 *literae, quae eorum gloriam immortalitatis memoria prosequantur.*

C. XXX. § 81. id non negat, i.e. that he killed him in self-defence; **id fateri,** that he killed him to save his country.

praemia laudis, 'Tribute of praise.' Cp. Arch. § 28 *mercedem laudis et gloriae.* Halm says that this would require *praemium* and takes it 'rewards for his merit,' a common enough meaning of the word, but cp. Balb. § 10 *praemia amplissimae dignitatis* (and Reid's note).

nisi vero, cp. on § 17.

sed tamen, v. on § 59.

si minus, practically = *si non,* cp. *quo minus*; hence the French 'més-,' our 'mis-.'

cecidisset grata, cp. Ad Quint. I. 3, 1 *a te mihi semper omnia honesta et iucunda ceciderunt. Accido* and *gratus* or *ingratus* are often thus coupled, e.g. Planc. 58.

laetarentur, subj., v. on *posset* § 71.

propter quem, v. on § 58.

§ 82. omnes fuimus, i.e. the list enumerated in § 83, *Ahala, Nasica, Opimius, Marius, Cicero.*

sine meis maximis &c., 'that the venture would not involve a terrible struggle for myself.' For the possessive pronoun cp. *sine meo periculo* Phil. I. 38, and elsewhere. Livy XXXI. 81 *cum magnis nostris cladibus,* 'with great disaster to us.' So *nulla sua invidia* § 40 of this speech.

§ 83. conscientia, v. on § 61.

fortuna p. R. et vestra felicitas. In § 6 we had *felicitas p. R.* The two words are the same thing objectively and subjectively considered. Cp. Ad Herenn. IV. 20 *fortuna felicitatem dedit.* It must be remembered that *fortuna* has little or nothing of the idea of our good luck. 'The ancients understood by fortune an inscrutable divine agency, as we do by providence.'

imperii nostri magnitudo &c. is a proof of the existence of *fortuna* : **sol ille** &c. of *di immortales*.

caeli signorumque motus, the sky itself, as often, is supposed to move.   Cp. De Nat. II. 97 *tam certos caeli motus, tam ratos astrorum ordines.*

vicissitudines rerum atque ordines.   'The alternation and order which prevail in nature.'   The plural *ordines*, because each *res* has its own *ordo*, v. Näg. § 12.   Cp. De Nat. II. 15 *in tantis motionibus, tantisque vicissitudinibus, tam multarum rerum atque tantarum ordinibus.*

sacra, 'worship,' and everything connected with it, a wider word than *caerimoniae*, 'ritual.'

C. XXXI. § 84.   neque in his corporibus &c.   'Nor can it be that, *while* in these bodies of ours and in this frail condition there exists a something which has activity and consciousness, that something does not exist in the vast and glorious revolutions of the universe,' a good instance of a well-known construction by which a contradiction or contrast between two ideas is expressed by simply placing them side by side.   The special case exemplified here, where the contradiction is declared to be impossible by a negative which applies to both of its parts, is not so common in Latin as in Greek, where the use of μὲν makes the construction far clearer: v. Madv. § 438, Mayor Phil. II. 110, also Madv. Grk. Syn. § 189.   Cp. the English 'you cannot eat your cake and have it.'   We have much the same construction with the same thought in Leg. II. 7 *neminem oportet esse tam stulte arrogantem, ut in se rationem et mentem putet inesse, in caelo mundoque non putet.*

non putant, they do not believe *in it*, cp. *deos non putare*, οὐ νομίζειν τοὺς θεούς.

haec ipsa, 'at this very moment.'

felicitates, a rare plural, used perhaps for symmetry (*concinnitas*) with *opes*.   Cp. *vigiliis et quietibus* Sall. Cat. 15, and perhaps De Sen. § 78 *tot artes tantae scientiae, tot inventa* (though *scientiae* may be gen.): Plaut. Most. 348 *summis opibus atque industriis*, v. Dräger Hist. Syn. § 7.

primum—Where is the 'secondly'? Not, as Eberhard, in *nisi forte hoc etiam casu* &c. § 86, which introduces a working of providence of a different order, but in *nec vero non* &c. at the beginning of C. XXXII., which shews how providence secondly infatuated Cl.'s followers.

mentem iniecit, the well-known thought of *quem deus per-*

dere vult dementat. Cp. Cat. iii. 22 *nisi ab dis immortalibus huic tantae audaciae consilium esset ereptum* (and Wilkins' note : the whole passage is similar to this).

habiturus esset. Poynton 'would have been likely to enjoy,'—rather 'hoped to have,' 'was going to have.' The sense is the same as if C. had written *si vicisset, habiturus erat.* The subjunctive *esset* is the result of dependence upon another subjunctive.

§ 85. **ne mediocri quidem cura,** 'not even any ordinary providence.'

religiones, concrete, 'sacred places,' below abstract, 'sanctities.'

ius suum retinuisse. Cp. Balb. 31 *sui quemque iuris et retinendi et dimittendi esse dominum.*

obrutae, i.e. by Clodius. The temples were spared at the destruction of the city, Livy i. 29.

sociae et aequales, 'partners in honour and antiquity,' though according to Roman legend Alba was actually older.

praeceps amentia, 'in the torrent of his madness.' The phrase is more fully expressed Verr. v. 121 *praeceps amentia ferebare,* cp. De Domo 141 *praeceps scelere.*

substructionum, v. on § 53.

irae, a correction for *arae* of the MSS., which is clearly wrong, as the *vos* addressed in *vestrae* are the *arae et luci.* The Cologne MS. omits the word. For the alliteration in the sentence v. on § 30.

Iuppiter Latiaris...edito monte...lacus, v. Classical Dict. on Alba.

§ 86. **nisi forte,** another *reductio ad absurdum.* 'If you ascribe it to mere chance that he fell in the presence of the *Albana sacra,* you must, to be consistent, suppose that his being wounded *ante sacrarium Bonae deae* was a chance also. But this is too much to be believed.'

videretur, 'he seems,' v. on *esset* § 11.

C. xxxii. **nec vero non,** 'surely too,' v. on *primum* in § 84.

sine imaginibus &c., a description of the concomitants of a funeral much the same as in § 33, but with further details, *cantu* i.e. the *cornicines* and *tibicines*—*ludi* i.e. the gladiatorial games—*lamentis* i.e. the dirge sung by the *praeficae.*

sine funere. What does *funus* mean here? The run of the sentence hardly allows us to suppose with Purton that it is 'a comprehensive term, including all the rest.' Others take it = *feretrum*, but the evidence of such phrases as *funere efferre*, *funus ducere* is not convincing; and in the passage quoted from Suet. Dom. 15 *evenit ut repentina tempestate, deiecto funere semiustum cadaver discerperent canes*, the word *semiustum* goes to shew that *funus* rather = *rogus* (or *rogus* + *cadaver*). Servius on Aen. II. 539 says *funus est iam ardens cadaver, quod dum portatur exsequias dicimus, crematum reliquias.* So here *funus* may mean 'the funeral proper,' i.e. the burning, and *sine funere* = *semustilatus* of § 33, as *ambureretur* in this section, cp. *insepulti* § 91.

celebritas. Purton gives 'concourse,' but a concourse was the one element of an ordinary funeral which Cl. had. L. and S. give 'solemnity,' quoting this passage and Livy xxx. 38.

clarissimorum virorum formas, i.e. the *imagines*, v. § 33.

aliquid decoris afferre, *aliquid* in a negative sentence, because *aliquid afferre* is a stereotyped phrase. Dräger I. § 46. So *aliquid profecerat* § 88.

mortem lacerari, *mortem* for *mortuum* a poetical (Halm says colloquial) usage, v. examples in L. and S., and Pro Sest. § 83 *eius igitur vitam quisquam spoliandam ornamentis esse dicet, cuius mortem ornandam monumento sempiterno putaretis;* but *mortem lacerare* is a far bolder phrase than *mortem ornare.*

loco, i.e. in the senate-house.

in quo vita esset damnata, cp. *cuius supplicio senatus solemnes religiones expiandas saepe censuit,* § 73. But perhaps *vita* may mean 'conduct during life.' Cp. Verr. Act. I. 10 *istius vitam iampridem omnium voluntate iudicioque damnatam.*

§ 87. **decreta,** cp. § 73 (quoted in last note).

vexarat in tribunatu senatum, cp. Sest. 66 *quis* (i.e. during Cl.'s tribunate) *provinciam, quis pecuniam, quis legationem a senatu petebat,* cp. § 73 and notes.

gesta, 'measures *taken*,' not 'measures *passed.*' *Resciderat* 'had undone,' i.e. by banishing their author.

domum mei fratris incenderat. Nov. 57, v. Att. IV. 3.

instabat, urgebat, cp. Pro Planc. § 48 *etiam atque etiam insto atque urgeo.*

capere, 'contain,' Greek χωρεῖν. From this sense of the word comes our 'measures of capacity.'

incidebantur, i.e. *in aes.* Laws were engraved *after* being passed. C. means that Cl. was sure of being praetor and of passing his laws.

quae nos servis nostris, v. note on *servos nostros* § 89.

adamasset, L. and S. give 'love deeply,'—rather 'learn to love,' 'fall in love with,' v. Reid on Acad. II. 9. Here the idea is that Cl. gratified every whim however new. So *addubito* 'to come to doubt,' R. 1835.

quod quidem...quod non putaret, cp. Cat. IV. 16 *servus est nemo qui modo tolerabili condicione sit servitutis, qui non audaciam civium perhorrescat.* R. 1692. Cp. the subj. here after *qui quidem* with the indic. in § 3.

§ 88. **illum ipsum**, i.e. Pompey.

potentiam, v. on § 12.

in meo casu, i.e. my exile.

C. XXXIII. **credo**, v. on § 36.

circumscripsisset, 'would have curtailed his powers.' The senate claimed to be able to do this by a decree *si quis aliter fecisset, eum contra rempublicam facturum esse,* v. Phil. II. 53, Att. VII. 9 (and Tyrrell's note).

ne cum solebat quidem, i.e. according to Asconius, at the time of the *Bona Dea* scandal, early in 61, when he was quaestor elect, but had not gone to his province. Better perhaps in 57, between his tribunate in 58 and aedileship in 56.

aliquid profecerat, sc. cp. *aliquid afferre* § 86 (and note).

§ 89. **consules suos**, 'consuls after his heart,' i.e. Hypsaeus and Scipio. Cp. Piso 27 *Gabinius se collegit contra suum Clodium.* So *venti sui* 'favourable winds,' *ver suum, sopor suus* 'the spring,' 'the sleep they love' in Horace and Virgil.

virtutem consularem, cp. *haec tanta virtus* § 101.

oppressisset, possideret, obs. the tenses: *oppressio* comes first and is a single action: *possessio* comes after and is permanent.

lege nova &c., cp. § 33 and 87 *leges quae nos nostris servis addicerent.* Asconius' explanation is that C. alludes to a proposal to allow the *libertini* to vote in all the tribes instead of in four city tribes. This explanation, has, I believe, been generally accepted, but while it is probable that the Clodian laws included this familiar plank of the radical platform, I can hardly think it covers the whole allusion. Twice over Cicero deliberately uses the word *servi*, and while doing full justice to his powers of exaggeration, we may still ask why he wantonly insults the great *ordo libertinorum*, whose loyalty he praises in Cat. IV. 16 and of whom he says in Sest. 97 *sunt etiam libertini optimates.* Moreover, 'he would have made our slaves his freedmen' is a strange hyperbole for 'he would have given our freedmen a better status.' On the other hand, this does not seem a case in which Asconius' opinion is of overwhelming weight. The Clodian laws were only *schemes with which Clodius was credited.* Many reports of these would be current. The most absurd report is the one which Cicero would be most likely to adopt and which Asconius would be least likely to find in his authorities. Altogether I do not see why we should not suppose that Cicero credits Clodius with a scheme affecting the status of *slaves.* What the scheme was we do not know, because Clodius did not live to propose it, and perhaps never even imagined it. Peyron suggested that he proposed to give citizenship to the lower class of Freedmen, who not having been emancipated by one of the three statutory modes had no citizenship, though protected by the praetor in the actual enjoyment of freedom. But I venture to ask whether it is impossible to take the words *literally.* In this case Clodius is credited with a scheme for manumitting slaves under some conditions without the consent of their masters, and making himself their *patronus.* Laws *did* exist at Rome enforcing the manumission of slaves and providing for the forfeiture of the patron's rights (v. Dict. Ant. *servus* and *patronus*). [In Dion Cassius 39, 23 Clodius is said to have been anxious that the 'slaves from Cyprus' should be called *Claudii.*] Once more we must remember that we have to consider not what Clodius actually proposed, but what Cicero thought he possibly might have proposed.

quae...Clodianis, possibly a gloss.

homo)(virum. Cp. Pro Sest. 89 *praestantissimus vir profligatissimo homini,* Pro Cael. 12 *utebatur hominibus improbis multis, et quidem optimis se viris deditum esse simulabat. Vir* is rarely used with bad qualities. *Homo* on the other hand is often used with complimentary adjectives, but very rarely with *fortis.* For other cases of juxtaposition of the two words, where the contrast is less strongly marked, v. Wilkins on De Or. III. 13.

rem publicam nullam haberetis. 'Not a vestige of the commonwealth (or 'constitution') would be left to us.' The phrase is perhaps colloquial, as in *nullus venio, nullus discedo,* v. Tyrrell on the Letters vol. I. p. 61. So *nulla est respublica,* De Off. II. 3, Cat. III. 25: *nulla esse iudicia* Clu. §77. Compare especially De Or. I. 38 *libertinos in urbanas tribus transtulit, quod nisi fecisset, rempublicam quam nunc vix tenemus iam diu nullam haberemus,* a passage which may perhaps be thought to support Asconius' interpretation of the *lex nova* above.

§ 90. **ille vero consul,** 'and what is more as consul.' The supposition of Cl. alive and praetor involved also his being consul in the course of time.

qui...duce, i.e. Cl. burnt the senate-house, led by Sextus. Surely a very strange expression. The Cologne MS. has *cui mortuo unus ex suis satellitibus curiam incenderit*, v. Clark p. XLIII.

templum, cp. § 66.

sanctitatis, amplitudinis, *sanctus* and *amplus* are standing epithets of the senate. For the former cp. Cat. I. § 9 *sanctissimo consilio*, Virg. Aen. I. 421 *sanctumque senatum*, Hor. Odes IV. 5, 4 *sancto concilio patrum:* whether the epithet meant 'holy in conduct,' or 'sacred,' the Romans probably did not know themselves.

mentis, to be taken as well as *consilii* with *publici*, cp. De Har. Resp. 58 *senatum ipsum principem salutis, mentisque publicae.* Translate 'intelligence.'

consilii publici, here as in many other cases it may be doubted whether the phrase means the 'state-council' or 'national policy,' 'statesmanship.' Probably the latter, as the three other nouns with which it is connected are abstract nouns.

portus &c., cp. De Off. II. 26 *regum, populorum, nationum portus erat et refugium senatus.* In Verr. v. 126 the *iudices* are the *portus, arx, ara, sociorum.*

imperita, v. on § 62.

signifer, the word is generally coupled with *dux* and *princeps*, e.g. Pro Mur. 50, Planc. 74: it does not imply as our 'standard-bearer' a 'lieutenant,' but a 'leader of men.' As *ustor*, Sextius Clodius was *unus*, as *signifer* he would have had Clodius' men at his back.

funesta, desecrated by the presence of a corpse.

§ 91. **et**, 'and then,' of indignation and surprise, cp. Virg. Georg. II. 433, Aen. VI. 807, Näg. 192, 2 d.

de Appia via, v. § 18.

furiae, sometimes *Poenae*, the incarnation of the dead man's vengeance. For the plural cp. *Manes.*

falcibus, i.e. *falcibus muralibus*, instruments used for pulling down walls &c.

ad Castoris. Some suggest that as the temple of Castor was used as a treasury the object of the assailants was plunder. This seems unnecessary. The temple of Castor occupied a strong position in the Forum and was often attacked and occupied in street conflicts. In B.C. 58 it was held by a Clodian mob, who knocked away the steps to strengthen the position, cp. Pro Sest. 34, Piso 11.

volitarunt, generally used by Cicero in an unfavourable sense, sometimes of arrogant and swaggering people, cp. De Or. I. 173, Cat. II. 5, sometimes of rioters and rebels, Cat. II. 15 *Catilinam in armis volitare.* Sest. 9 *cum illa coniuratio palam armata volitaret.* It is especially common with *toto foro, per forum.* For metaphors from flying v. Näg. 132.

disturbari, 'broken up,' stronger than 'disturb,' so frequently of demolishing buildings.

silentio, i.e. and therefore the attack of the Clodians was the more unjustifiable.

vir et in re publica &c. The compliments to Caelius like *silentio* bring out the wickedness of the Clodians in interrupting such a man. But C. is also no doubt glad to make an opportunity for gracefully complimenting his chief supporter in the case, v. Intr. p. xxii.

in re publica, i.e. as a statesman: further explained by *bonorum...deditus.* **in suscepta causa**, i.e. in defending individuals; further explained by *in hac Milonis...fide.*

auctoritas, the will of a superior whose wishes in themselves command respect. *Voluntas* that of ordinary people. But in § 94 the *boni* have or had *auctoritas.*

C. xxxiv. § 92. Here begins the *peroratio.*

de causa, i.e. that Cl. was an insidiator §§ 24—71. **extra causam**, that his death was a blessing to the state §§ 72—91.

exposco. Purton gives 'claim as his due.' The word does not occur elsewhere in C., but the instances quoted from Livy and Caesar in L. and S. do not support this meaning, nor does it suit the humble tone of the passage. *Imploro et exposco* is only another instance of the duplication of synonyms, which we see in *orem et obtester, exanimant et interimunt, cedam atque abibo.*

nostro omnium fletu, so Cat. I. 9 *de nostro omnium interitu*, id. IV. 4 *vestram omnium caedem.* But *nostrum omnium* or rather *omnium nostrum* is far more common in Cicero.

nullam lacrimam, C. endeavours to construe what to Milo's contemporaries seemed insolent defiance into a sign of heroism. A dry-eyed defendant was regarded in a Roman court, much as a laughing defendant would be in an English court. Milo's attitude greatly helped his condemnation. Plut. Cic. 35.

condicione atque fortuna. Not as Purton 'where the standing and fate of the lowest class is concerned,' as though their *condicio et fortuna* depended on the contest, or the feeling of their spectators, but 'in the case of persons whose position and lot is that of the lowest class.' Cp. Balb. § 24 *servos, quorum ius, fortuna, condicio infima est*, De Off. I. 41 *est autem infima condicio et fortuna servorum.*

fortis atque animosos, for the courage displayed by the gladiators, v. Dict. Ant. and passages quoted (esp. Cic. Tusc. II. 41), Mayor on Juv. III. 36.

ipsos = *ultro*, subject to *offerentes.*

§ 93.   **intersum** = *audio*, cp. De Sen. 7 *saepe enim interfui querellis aequalium meorum.*

patria, Rome, not Italy.   The Greeks and Romans thought of a native city rather than a native land, cp. Phil. XI. 10 *moenibus patriae.*   Leg. Agr. II. 86 *Romam communem patriam nostrum omnium.*   Though born at Lanuvium M. was a citizen of Rome and thus Rome was his *patria*, cp. § 102 *hic qui me procreavit locus.*

quoquo modo &c., 'however ill she has served me.'

propter me, v. on § 58.

si non licuerit = *si non licebit.   Potuero, noluero, licuerit* are used for the future, because the possibility, lawfulness &c. of the action must be proved before it can take place, Zumpt 510, Madv. 340, obs. 3.

bona...mala re publica, 'good government,' 'mis-government.'

at, 'at any rate,' fully illustrated in L. and S.

quam primum, we should expect *primam* which Garatoni and others read, declaring the adverb to be bad Latin.   Cat. III. 15 *quod mihi primum post hanc urbem conditam togato contigit*, and other instances quoted there by Halm are not exact parallels, as *primum* means there 'for the first time.' But v. Madv. De Fin. I. 44 on *solum* for *solus.*

bene moratam...civitatem.   *Civitas* is used more with reference to the social and moral condition of a community—*respublica* to its government and constitution, cp. De Sen. 63 *ut quaeque (civitas) optime morata est* (v. Nettleship ' Contributions,' *civitas*).

§ 94.   **mihi**, the dative of the agent is found more frequently in Cicero with *susceptus* than with any other past participle, e.g. Pro Man. 71, Sulla 28 (Dräger Hist. Syn. 189).

suscepti, Cicero more often joins *O* with the accusative, v. Reid on De Sen. 66.

tribunus plebis, i.e. in 57, the year of C.'s recall.

extinctum, 'annihilated,' cp. De Off. III. 2 *senatu extincto iudiciisque deletis* (by Antony).

tui, not so much referring to Cicero's equestrian origin, as to his constant political attachment to the knights.

voces Italiae, cp. § 39.

vox atque defensio, 'eloquent advocacy.'

C. xxxv. § 95. **plebem et infimam multitudinem**, note the emphatic position v. Näg. 148. But the repetition of *plebem* in *eam* makes this passage more emphatic than the others there quoted. Cp. *ille cessisset, is qui ita natus est* § 68, v. Madv. 489.

fecisse ut flecteret...**deleniret**, v. Madv. § 481, Zumpt § 619. Though called a periphrasis by the grammarians, the construction is perhaps somewhat stronger than the simple verb and calls especial attention to the ease or difficulty, agreeableness or disagreeableness &c., of the action. Thus it is several times used with *invitus, non invitus, libenter*, e.g. De Sen. 42, De Am. 4. In Cat. iii. 7 *negavi me esse facturum ut de periculo publico non ad consilium publicam rem integram deferrem*, 'I said I could not think of not reporting &c.' Pro Clu. § 111 *facite ut recordemini* 'do recollect.' So here 'he has *managed to* soothe them by his three fortunes, as well as guide them by his personal merits.'

tribus...**patrimoniis**, v. Introduction, p. x.

muneribus, sc. *gladiatoriis*. "Strictly speaking gladiatorial exhibitions and no others were called *munera*." Reid on Sulla 54. So Caesar Bell. Civ. iii. 23 says of Milo in B.C. 48 *magnis muneribus datis gladiatoriae familiae reliquias habebat*. In his letters (Ad Quint. iii. 8 and 9) C. deplores Milo's extravagance.

vestras et vestrorum ordinum, i.e. acc. to Halm, the knights and *Tribuni Aerarii*, the senate having just been mentioned: but perhaps the words *senatus...perspectam* give the *official* expressions of good will from the senate as a whole, while those of individual senators are included in the words that follow.

occursationes &c., 'your constant attendance on him, your demonstrations, your friendly expressions.' *Occursatio* embraces (1) *salutatio* or attendance at levées, (2) *deductio* escorting him from his house to the Forum or Campus, (3) *adsectatio* or attendance on other occasions. Cp. Commentariolum Petitionis §§ 34—37.

quemcumque cursum, cp. Aen. iv. 653 *quem dederat cursum Fortuna peregi*.

§ 96. **vocem praeconis**, i.e. the election had been practically completed but the herald had not formally announced the result, when it was interrupted, cp. § 25.

haec, 'the present proceedings'=*novi iudicii nova forma* of § 1.

facinoris suspicionem, 'suspicion of some villainy,' i.e. plots against the state or Pompey. *Facti crimen* 'the charge of the deed,' i.e. the deed for which he is arraigned=*crimen Clodianum* of § 67.

honori a civibus, obs. the *a* after a substantive, so with *spes, metus, periculum, insidiae,* and not unfrequently after *inire gratiam,* e.g. Sest. 132 *ut a me inierit gratiam.*

beneficio vincere, 'to outdo in conferring benefits.' *Beneficium* being used for 'doing kindness' in general rather than a single kind action. So *officium* for *officia.* The same phrase occurs in Planc. 81 (speaking of ingratitude) *nihil tam inhumanum quam committere ut beneficio non dicam indignus sed victus esse,* where Holden explains 'overpowered by the magnitude of the service, so that one does not so much as attempt to requite it.' But the explanation given above seems to me much simpler, cp. Eur. Herc. Fur. 342 ἀρετῇ σε νικῶ θνητὸς ὢν θεὸν μέγαν. [The same may, I think, be said of *beneficiis vincere* Sall. Jug. 9 where Merivale translates 'win over by good offices': still more clearly in id. 102 *in pectus tuum demitte nunquam populum Romanum beneficiis victum.*]

§ 97. sed tamen, i.e. though it is true that rewards are not the brave man's object.

si esset, a sudden change to historic time; maintained down to the end of the section, v. on § 11.

consolaretur, 'compensate for,' v. Exx. in L. and S.

ut absentes adessemus, cp. De Am. § 23 of true friends, *quocirca et absentes adsunt et egentes abundant, et imbecilli valent, et quod difficilius dictu est, mortui vivunt.*

cuius gradibus &c., cp. Paradoxa i. 11 *quibus tandem gradibus Romulus escendit in caelum; iisne quae isti bona appellant, an rebus gestis atque virtutibus?* So also Leges ii. 19 *olla propter quae datur homini ascensus in caelum,* i.e. the qualities which win men immortality.

§ 98. vetustas, generally taken as 'future age,' 'posterity,' a use for which no real parallel is adduced: for Virg. Aen. x. 792 *si qua fidem tanto est operi latura vetustas* probably means, 'if the lapse of time can ever make such a deed believed,' i.e. such a story can only be believed of ancient and heroic times (v. Papillon). In Pro Deiot. 37 *quae vetustas obruet?* Phil. xii. 12 *quae vetustas tollet?* the word also means 'lapse of time.' I do not feel sure that the word is not used here in the ordinary sense of 'the past,' (cp. e.g. Archias 14 *plena est exemplorum vetustas*) or rather 'the records and traditions of the past.' Each future age, Cicero then means, will have its *vetustas*, and this will always include Milo's story. If this is right 'history will never cease to speak of me,' would be a fair equivalent.

faces invidiae meae subiciantur, cp. § 75.

omni in hominum coetu &c., i.e. Milo is honoured (1) in every gathering, whether the honour takes the form of *gratiarum actio* formal vote of thanks or *gratulatio* simple expressions of joy and congratulation, (2) in all private conversations between individuals. For *gratias agere*)(*gratulationes* cp. Phil. xiv. 13 *sive in communi gaudio populi Romani uni gratulabantur, magnum iudicium, sive uni gratias agebant, eo maius, sive utrumque nihil magnificentius cogitari potest.*

omitto, evidently a relapse into Cicero's own words, v. on § 75. The resumption of M.'s speech is marked by *inquit.*

et actos et institutos, 'whether already celebrated, or appointed to be celebrated.'

opinor. The date is perfectly exact and C. knew it to be so. The addition of *opinor* is a natural rhetorical device, to affect an air of unpremeditation. The accuracy with which C. remembered the date of Cl.'s death is shown by the fact that in two of his letters Att. v. 13, vi. 1, he dates events as happening on the 650th and 765th days after Clodius' death.

eǎ, agreeing with *fama.* Others *eā* correlative with *qua.*

de illo, i.e. *interitu Clodii.*

C. xxxvi. § 99. **cum isto animo es.** *cum* with the indicative in the sense of *quod* is found in earlier writers: in Cicero's time only with words expressing joy and thankfulness, R. 1725, Madv. de Fin. i. § 10. The other instances quoted are Ad Fam. ix. 14 *gratulor tibi cum tantum vales apud Dolabellam,* Ad Fam. xiii. 24 *gratias ago cum tantum litterae meae potuerunt,* Sall. Jug. 102 *magna nobis laetitia est, cum te talem virum di monuere.*

eriperis, more pathetic than *eripieris* or *ereptus eris.* Cicero feels the separation already beginning: so *divellor* above.

illa tamen ad consolandum querella, 'the last poor means of consolation, complaint.' *tamen* is often used thus, with an ellipse of a concessive clause equivalent to 'little though that is,' 'though all else be gone.' Cp. e.g. Clu. 22 *eum filium quem tamen unum ex multis fortuna reliquum esse voluisset,* 'the one poor survivor.' Caesar B. G. i. 32 *quod reliquis tamen facultas fugae daretur, Sequanis vero...omnes cruciatus essent perferendi,* 'to the others at any rate the opportunity was granted.'

Other instances in Cicero are Rosc. Am. 8, 104, Sest. 63, Caec. 48.

ut iis irasci &c., substantival clause explaining *querella*.

aliquando, Halm 'on several occasions.' Perhaps rather 'on a single occasion,' the word being used in preference to *unquam* to mark the antithesis to *semper* as in § 66 *timebat omnia Pompeius ne vos aliquid timeretis*.

nullum umquam &c. 'No pain that you can inflict, will ever be so great (and yet what pain can equal the present) no not even this pain can be great enough to make me forget' &c. After *ne hunc quidem ipsum* understand *tantum* (or *ita*) *inuretis*. C. begins by saying that no future grief can make him forget: as this implies that some future grief may equal the present, he substitutes 'this present.' Observe that the first *tantus* 'great enough to make me forget,' has no reference to the second *tantus* 'as great as the present.'

inuretis, v. on § 33.

quae oblivio, *cuius rei oblivio,* Edd. Perhaps rather the antecedent of the relative lies in the verb *obliviscor*.

si...aliquid, v. on § 67.

offendistis, 'fall foul of,' 'find cause of offence,' not a common use of the word, which far more often means 'to give offence.' The same use is found in Pro Caec. 104 *si quid in homine offendendum sit*, 'if anything personal ought to be a matter of objection,' (perhaps also in Ad Qu. Fr. I. 1, 4, 14). L. and S. quote Caesar B. C. II. 32 *si Caesarem probatis, in me offenditis.* The same meaning is implied in *offensus* = 'offensive.'

vixero, 'I shall end my life,' cp. the famous *vixerunt* of Cicero at the execution of the Catilinarians.

si quid acciderit, v. on § 58.

§ 100.   **pietatis,** 'gratitude.'

inimicitias...appetivi, more fully expressed De Har. Resp. § 7 *inimicitias non solum suscepit, verum etiam appetivit.*

supplicem abieci, cp. Pro Sest. § 58 *hunc Cn. Pompeius, cum in suis castris supplicem abiectum vidisset, erexit.*

in communionem tuorum temporum, 'to share in your adversities,' v. on *tempori* § 2.

dimicatio capitis, v. on *honoris contentio* § 42.

deposco, 'I claim it for myself,' more often *deposco mihi*.

augeatis in salute. Milo's 'salus' *involves* the increase. So *in confessione honores adsequeretur* § 81.

aut...videatis, 'or else to recognise that his destruction involves the overthrow of these kindnesses,' a disproportionate alternative standing for 'or else they will be overthrown,' v. Näg. § 161.

C. xxxvii. § 101. **quodam**, v. note on § 21.

exilium ibi esse, i.e. remaining at Rome now, would be true exile; or perhaps 'exile is an impossibility, for virtue can find room everywhere.'

naturae finem. Purton translates 'death is the termination of our being,' for which might be quoted the description of death as *dissolutio naturae*, De Fin. v. 31, Leges i. 31. But the general use of *natura* in Cicero points rather to taking the words as 'the end appointed by nature.' *Poenam* perhaps also to be taken with *naturae*, cp. Pro Clu. § 29 (where taking a less Stoical view) C. says *quem leges exsilio, natura morte multavit.* Compare also Phil. xi. 3 *mortem naturae poenam putat*, (though some Edd. bracket *poenam*). For the whole sentiment cp. Cat. iv. 7 *mortem ab dis immortalibus non esse supplicii causa constitutam, sed aut necessitatem naturae aut laborum ac miseriarum quietem.*

procreavit, cp. on *patria* § 93.

haec tanta virtus, cp. *virtutem consularem* § 89.

§ 102. **per hos**, the Jury as representing the *boni*, cp. on § 4.

abes, i.e. as Caesar's *legatus* in Gaul.

temporum illorum, i.e. the events connected with C.'s banishment.

mene non potuisse, not the exclamatory inf. though that is common enough in Cic. but dependent on *respondebo.*

quae est grata gentibus non potuisse. This, the reading of the best MSS. obviously does not construe. One MS. (S) has *quae est grata gentibus. A quibus non potuisse? ab iis qui &c.*, which was the reading generally received by earlier editors. Madv. (Opusc. Ac. i. 155) objects (1) that *gentibus* is too bald for *gentibus omnibus* (but v. on § 30), (2) want of MS. authority, (3) that C. would not speak of protecting M. *from* the Jury. Recent editors have followed Madvig in admitting a lacuna. Madvig himself conjectures *quae est grata gentibus omnibus. At quibus iudicantibus non potuisse? iis &c.* Halm and others *eam probari* instead of *iudicantibus*, which certainly suits better with *quo deprecante.*

quo deprecante? 'who was the intercessor?'

§ 103. **concepi**, not 'planned,' but 'was guilty of:' much the same as *admisi*, cp. Sull. 16 *quod flagitium Lentulus non*

*cum Antonio concepit, quod sine eodem illo Catilina facinus
admisit?*

indicia communis exitii, 'the evidences of a plot that
threatened national destruction.' *Exitium* is active cp. *quantum in illo...exitii fuerit* § 78. So in Sest. 145 we have *quid
tanto opere deliqui illo die cum ad vos indicia, literas, confes-
siones communis exitii detuli.* Note the zeugma in *extinxi*: we
must supply *res indicatas* out of *indicia.* [Perhaps the figure is
rather the kindred figure of *syllepsis*, for in Rosc. Am. § 107
indicii partem, indicium seems to = *res indicata.*]

C. xxxviii. **ne scelerate** &c., 'that words which are right
and good so far as spoken for Milo are sinful towards thee.'

§ 104. **conservandum a vobis.** Note the gerundive with abl.
and *ab.* The usage is said to be rare except in Cicero and with
him is mainly used with personal pronouns. Three explana-
tions are given (1) that it is used to avoid ambiguity (2) to
balance clauses (3) to lay more stress than is laid by the
dative on 'the activity of the agent.' All three may be true
in different passages. Nos. (1) and (3) will suit our passage,
for *vobis* might be taken as dative of advantage (so Zumpt
§ 651), and C. may mean 'you the *boni ex amplissimis ordinibus*
are bound to save him, if no one else will.' The student who
wishes to investigate the usage may refer to the following,
Roby Pref. to Vol. ii. p. lxxv, do. § 1147, Reid on Balb. § 7,
Sulla § 23, Zumpt § 651, Dräg. Hist. Syn. i. § 189.

luerit, 'let him continue to have paid,' 'well that he has
paid.'

patriae natus, more fully *non sibi sed patriae natus,* cp.
Mur. § 83. The sentiment comes originally from Plato Ep. ix.
ad Archytam which C. quotes, De Off. i. 22, De Fin. ii. 45.

si forte, 'possibly,' εἰ τύχοι (Munro on Lucr. v. 720), cp. De
Or. iii. § 47, De Off. ii. § 70.

§ 105. **sed finis sit.** Quint. xi. 3, 173 quotes the passage
with the remark *illa mire facit in peroratione velut deficientis
dolore et fatigatione confessio.*

ADDITIONAL NOTES (chiefly on the text).

The chief MSS. for the speech are
P or the Turin Palimpsest.
E or Erfurtensis.
H (sometimes C) or Coloniensis.
T or Tegerniensis.
S or Salisburgensis.
B or Barberinus.

Of these P only remains for a few sections. E has usually been regarded as the most generally valuable authority. But since Mr Clark's recent collation of H, Anecdota Oxoniensia (Classical) Part VII., there has been something of a reaction in favour of that MS. But the question of the relative value of H and E may be regarded as still *sub judice*.

§ 2. **afferunt aliquid.** H and E add *terroris*. If *terroris* is omitted, *afferunt aliquid* should perhaps be taken closely with *ut* 'tend to make us fear,' cp. De Fato 8 *quid enim loci natura adfert ut in porticu Pompeii potius quam in campo ambulemus.*

iustissimi, so H, *illustrissimi* ETSB.

§ 5. **nobis duobus.** Garatoni bracketed *duobus*, referring *nobis* to the *optimates.*

§ 6. **sed si,** *sin* HE.

§ 7. **omni errore,** so HS, *terrore* ETB.

§ 8. **an est quisquam qui ignoret** &c. Cp. De Or. II. 105, 106 *nostrae fere causae, quae quidem sunt criminum, plerumque infitiatione defenduntur...Saepe etiam res non sit necne, sed qualis sit quaeritur; ut...Carboni tribuno plebis...P. Africanus de Ti. Graccho interroganti responderat, iure caesum videri: iure autem omnia defenduntur, quae sunt eius generis, ut aut oportuerit, aut licuerit; aut necesse fuerit aut imprudentia aut casu facta esse videantur.*

Ahala ille Servilius. This appears to be the only instance in the speeches of *nomen* and *cognomen* reversed, except where special significance is intended. Wilkins.

§ 12. **occisus est,** *occisus esset* H.

§ 14. H omits *quo* before *arma Saturnini* and *e* before *re publica.* Mr Clark approves this last as simplifying the construction, but it seems to me to weaken the sense.

§ 15. **non interitum putavit.** Nohl following Lehmann inserts *puniendum* after *interitum.*

§ 16. **illud ipse dicet.** Hedicke followed by Eberhard suggested *illud ipsum docet.* But the reading in the text yields excellent sense.

§ 17. **suorum sit interfectus.** Madvig corrected to *suorumst.* This he calls *necessaria correctio.* But the subj. seems natural enough, as the words are quoted from Milo's opponents.

proinde quasi Appius ille Caecus &c. Cp. Pro Cael. § 34, where the old Appius is represented as saying to his profligate descendant Clodia *ideo viam munivi ut eam tu alienis viris comitata celebrares.*

§ 23. **ei lecti,** so Garatoni, *electi* MSS.

§ 27. **quod erat dictator Lanuvi Milo,** bracketed by some editors as a gloss, unnecessarily.

§ 29. **impetum adversi, redarium occidunt.** So also Nohl. Most editors have *impetum, adversi redarium occidunt,* thus dividing the attackers into two parties.

§ 31. **ut ne sit inpune.** Mr Poynton takes *impune = impunitus* quoting Att. i. 16, 13 *ut qui nummos in tribus pronuntiarit, si non dederit, impune sit.* But in Tacitus, where it is fairly common *impune esse* appears to be regularly applied to the deed not the doer, Ann. i. 72, ii. 52, iii. 28, xii. 54.

§ 32. **in his personis.** I have followed what I suppose to be the meaning of Dr Reid's note on Sulla § 8. "*Persona* is strictly the mask used by actors when representing a typical character on the ancient stage. Hence *persona* came to mean 'character' implying always that the individual in connexion with whom it is used is one of a class." But I have some doubts of the truth of this rule. It is hard to see for instance how it can be applied in De Off. i. 107. In our own passage I doubt whether *in his personis* means more than 'in the case of these individuals.' Though it is generally true that *persona* does not = our 'person' (v. Reid l. c. and Ramsay on Clu. § 78), there are cases even in Cicero where it does mean 'person concerned.' I mean that when we are speaking of a case or a rule or a right &c., the human beings concerned thereby may be called *personae* without any thought of their character. Cp. Pro Cael. 30 *duo crimina in quibus una atque eadem persona versatur.* Flacc. 45 *omni et personarum genere et litterarum.* De Or. III. 53 *ut rerum, ut personarum dignitates ferunt.* Ad Fam. III. 5 *neque enim obscuris personis, nec parvis in causis res agetur.*

nec cuperent reprimere si possent. So Madvig for MSS. *nec si cuperent reprimere possent.*

§ 37.   **intentata,** *intento* also occurs Rosc. Am. 101 (omitted by Merguet).

§ 39.   **concurrerent,** *concurreret* H.   So many editors.

§ 43.   **cum se ille,** *quin se ille* ET, *qui se ille* H, *qui se* S. Mr Clark suggests that the clause is a gloss taking its construction from *dubitandum.*

§ 44.   **dubitarit,** so quoted by the rhetor Severianus.   MSS. *dubitaret.*

cogitarit, so ET, *cogitaret* HS.   The MSS. of Severianus differ.

§ 46.   **Interamnas,** *Interamnis* SB, *Interamnanus* HET.

cuius…Romae, omit H and Asconius.   Possibly a scholium which has crept into the text.

§ 50.   **ibi,** omit HS.

§ 51.   **ad Albanum,** *ad se in Albanum* H.

§ 53.   Perhaps take *'facile'* with *'mille'* rather than as in note, v. Wilkins on De Or. III. 60.

§ 56.   **semper ille,** *ille* omitted by Garatoni as *minime aptum Miloni.*

§ 59.   **de servis…Clodium,** possibly to be bracketed as a scholium, v. Clark p. XLII.

domini morte, *dominis* HS.   So Nohl.

§ 67.   **exaudire,** so Asconius.   MSS. *audire.*

§ 69.   **vide,** HE *vides.*

§ 79.   **nempe haec…P. Clodi.**   Mr Clark calls these 'very weak words,' and believes them to be an expansion of a gloss. But the words seem to me almost necessary to Cicero's argument, such as it is, v. note.

§ 83.   **fortuna populi Romani et vestra felicitas,** H omits *fortuna.*

§ 92.   **in infimi generis &c.,** *in* is read by most editors, but is not found in any good MS.

§ 93.   **propter,** so PH.   Other MSS. *per.*

§ 94.   **mihi,** so P.   Other MSS. and Quint. vi. 1, 27 *mei.*

§ 96.   **si haec contra se,** *haec arma* HE, *arma* is probably a gloss.

§ 100.   **habeo quod faciam,** MSS. *quid.*

§ 102.   **quae est grata** &c.   H has *quae est grā* (=*gratia*) *in gentibus.*   Mr Clark conjectures *quae est gratiis digna ingentibus* or *gratia ingenti omnibus in gentibus.*

ANALYSIS.

§§ 1, 2. The strange aspect of the court, the absence of the usual audience, and the presence of the troops startle me, I confess. § 2. But I am reassured by feeling that Pompey is so wise and just, that he means to protect, not to intimidate you. § 3. Remember that all real citizens are on Milo's side, the Clodian faction alone is against us, and their clamour should only encourage you to save the one man who can check them. § 4. Use then this opportunity of showing that you protect those that protect you. § 5. Indeed I never thought that a citizen like Milo could have anything to fear from a law court, however much he might be attacked in public meetings. § 6. And yet I do not ask you to lay too much stress on Milo's public career. I hope to prove to you that Clodius made a treacherous attack on Milo, and that Milo only killed him in self-defence. And, on this ground alone, shall I ask for an acquittal.

§ 7. First however I must answer certain preliminary objections.

I. It is said that no one who has committed homicide should be allowed to live.

What do those, who plead this, say to the acquittal of Horatius, (§ 8) or to Africanus' approval of the murder of Gracchus, or to the cases of Servilius Ahala and others? The story of Orestes, whom the goddess herself acquitted of matricide, has a profound truth. § 9. The same principle is laid down by the Twelve Tables which sanction the homicide of a burglar. Remember the story of Marius and the soldier. § 10. There is a law above written laws which justifies us in taking the life of another in defence of our own. Why, even the statute by forbidding to carry arms with murderous intent tacitly sanctions the use of arms in self-defence.

II. § 12. It is said that the Senate has declared against Milo. On the contrary it approved of his action. Munatius himself is my witness, for he told a public meeting that the Senate was at my beck and call. § 13. And you must not suppose that the Senate proposed this special commission on Clodius' death. It was not worth it. What, you ask then, did the Senate mean by voting that the fray in the Appian Road was an outrage to the state? Why, simply that all acts of violence are outrages to the state. § 14. Homicide in self-defence, and the murder of mischievous citizens are in one sense to be regretted. I voted for the motion myself, and all I meant was that the scandal required investigation, and if the Senate had had its own way, the matter would have been tried in the ordinary court.

III. § 15. But Pompey, you say, went further. He expressly mentioned the murder of Clodius, and proposed a special commission to deal with it. But what was the commission to try? Not the fact of the murder, for this was admitted, but whether the murder was justified or not. You see that the proposal, so far from condemning Milo, implies that he may deserve acquittal. § 16. What his motive in proposing a special commission was I must leave him to say. It cannot have been respect for Clodius. We had no special commission when Africanus and Drusus were murdered, (§ 17) and the reason is that murder is the same crime, whoever is the victim. I know some people say otherwise; they talk of Clodius being killed on the road which his ancestor built, (§ 18) but they did not say anything when he killed Papirius on the same road. But to come to more modern instances; Clodius plotted to kill Pompey and myself, (§ 19) but no special commission was ever proposed. § 20. But of course all these are not such valuable lives as Clodius; the whole country is mourning for him. § 21. No, Pompey was not thinking of Clodius' merits when he proposed this commission, but he had some far-seeing design; he wished to keep up the semblance of friendship to Clodius, but he knew that you might be trusted to acquit Milo. And so he did not exclude my friends from the jury; indeed, if he had, he could not have selected good men, (§ 22) and in moving that a consular should preside, and in choosing you particularly, Domitius, he meant to choose a safe man.

§ 23. Recapitulation. Therefore since admitted homicide does not necessarily imply crime, since the Senate has not prejudged the case, since Pompey has left a loophole for acquittal, and the judges and their president are impartial, the question to be decided is which plotted against the other? First for the facts.

Narratio. § 24. Clodius had postponed his candidature for the Praetorship a year. § 25. Then he found that Milo was likely to be elected consul for that year. He first canvassed against him, (§ 26) then he talked of killing him, (§ 27) then knowing that Milo was due at Lanuvium on the 18th of January he went on the 17th to his villa on the

Appian Road, though he had to leave an important meeting.
§ 28. Milo set out on the 20th in a family coach with his
wife. § 29. Clodius met and attacked him. Milo jumped
from his coach to defend himself, and in the fray, the slaves
of Milo, thinking that their master was dead, killed Clodius.

§§ 30, 31. Now if this story is true, Milo is justified. How
can I prove it?

Confirmatio. § 32. First for the argument from motive.
Clodius had good reasons for killing Milo, for he wanted a
free hand in his Praetorship. § 33. Don't you know what
laws he meant to propose? Then ask Sextus Clodius. § 34.
On the other hand if Milo killed Clodius he would lose the
chief glory of his public life. § 35. If you say Milo hated
Clodius it is not true. He only hated him as a citizen, but
Clodius did hate Milo who kept an action hanging over his
head.

§ 36. Then compare their life and character. Clodius
systematically used violence. Remember the time of my
banishment, and (§ 37) his other outrages. § 38. Milo never
attempted violence, and yet he had many opportunities, particularly at the time of my restoration, (§ 40) and quite lately
when Antonius nearly caught him.

§ 41. Is it likely then that he chose a time for the murder
when everything was unfavourable, and (§ 42) the slightest
mistake might lose him the chance for the consulship? § 43.
Again, the probable malefactor is the one who hopes for
impunity. That points to Clodius. § 44. But I have more
positive evidence than this. Clodius said before witnesses
that he would murder Milo. § 45. Again, Clodius could easily
learn about Milo's movements, for every one knew he had to
go to Lanuvium. § 46. Milo, on the other hand, knew
nothing of Clodius' movements. The Clodian witnesses themselves say that he did not mean to return to Rome and changed
his mind at the last moment. § 47. Well then, Milo cannot
have known his movements, nor can I, for some people say I
was mixed up in it. § 48. Oh, but you say, that if he intended
to stop in his villa, he did not mean treachery. Yes, if,—but I
don't believe it. The excuse was that he heard of the architect
Cyrus' death. § 49. But why should that make him hurry off
to Rome? Besides if Milo meant to waylay him, he would
have waited for him at some thieves' corner or between Aricia
and his Alban villa.

§§ 51, 52. Recapitulation of arguments up to this point.
§ 53. Look also at the place of meeting, just in front of the
high ground, on which Clodius' farm stood. § 54. Look also
at the equipment of the two, coach *v.* horse, wife *v.* no wife.
Look at Clodius' suspicious dawdling. § 55. Clodius too
had a few picked men, but Milo all his wife's maids and pages.

Why then, you say, did Milo get the best of it? Well, the traveller often beats the robber, and (§ 56) Milo was always on his guard against Clodius. Then there is the luck of war, and Clodius was stupid and drowsy after his lunch, and so fell into the hands of Milo's slaves. § 57. You ask why he emancipated those slaves! Afraid of their making disclosures under torture! Nonsense! they had nothing to disclose. The fact is admitted and its justice is not a question that can be settled by the rack. § 58. The real reason, and I have Cato's authority for saying this, was that the least he could do to show his gratitude was to enfranchise them. § 59. Well, but Clodius' slaves are being examined and making disclosures that tell against Milo. Very likely, but look at the position. Appius into whose possession they passed, had every opportunity for priming them. It was bad enough to ask for Milo's slaves, but this last is too much. § 60. Of course the slaves will say anything they are asked. A reliable sort of examination this!

§ 61. If you want more evidence, look at Milo's attitude after his return and how frankly he threw himself on the protection of the State! Was that like a guilty man? §§ 62, 63. Many people said he would go into exile, some talked of a repetition of Catiline. § 64. Then how courageously he bore the charges of conspiring! All sorts of stories were current. § 65. Pompey, I suppose was obliged to listen to them. Still, I do not think he need have listened to a story like that of the butcher Licinius. § 66. There were other charges as absurd as that of carrying a sword which Milo refuted by baring his thigh. § 67. And yet people still fear Milo! But it is your suspicions, Pompey, that make the jury's verdict doubtful. Can all these military preparations be intended to oppose Milo? § 68. Assuredly not, but only to cure the disorder of the state. If you would only have admitted Milo to an interview he would have proved his loyalty, or if you had refused to listen gone into exile with a solemn protest. This protest even now he makes. § 69. Some day the time will come when you will want his help and acknowledge its truth. § 70. And yet it is incredible that if Pompey had suspected Milo he should take legal measures against him ; rather he would have punished him at once. § 71. No, the law he proposed, and the presence of his soldiers both mean that you are left to give a verdict as your conscience directs.

Extra causam. § 72. And indeed I know that you approve of Clodius' death.

Milo might safely plead that he had killed a man guilty of sacrilege and incest, who banished me, thwarted the Senate, shut up Pompey in his own house, burnt the registers, (§ 74) committed numberless outrages on individuals, (§ 75) and threatened worse. You know this is true (§ 77) and therefore

if Milo had declared himself his murderer how grateful you
would have been! As it is how universal is the joy. § 78. We
all know that nothing would have been safe had he lived.
I do not fear that this should be thought the language of
personal spite. I hated him it is true, but so did all. § 79.
Consider it in this light. Suppose you, or Pompey could recall
him to life, would you do so? No. How absurd then that
you should sit, by a law of Pompey's proposing, to avenge his
death. § 80. Rather you should honour him, as the Greeks
honour tyrannicides. § 81. He would confess the deed if he had
done it, and if you failed to appreciate it, leave his ungrateful
country. § 82. Though indeed he who kills the enemies of
his country knows that he runs a risk, otherwise where would
be the merit? The country if grateful would no doubt reward
him. But the brave man does not fear ingratitude, for he is
content with his own conscience. § 83. But in all this can
be seen the working of that divine Providence of whose existence we are assured by the greatness of Rome, by the wonders
of nature, by our own souls. § 84. It was this Providence
which infatuated Clodius to attack Milo. § 85. The Alban
altars and the Latian Jupiter presided over his death. § 86.
Why, he fell close to the temple of the Bona Dea whom he had
outraged. The same Providence drove his followers to give
him the burial of a dog. § 87. Providence indeed had long
allowed him to rage unchecked. § 88. Milo was the only one
left who could restrain him. § 89. The Senate, the Consuls
would have been powerless against him. § 90. Why, even
his dead body could burn down the Senate House! and what
would he have done if alive?

Peroration. § 92. But I have said enough now. I ask you to
grant Milo the mercy he is too brave to ask. Grant it him all
the more for his bravery, as we spare the gladiator who does not
fear death. § 93. He often tells me he is contented to leave
his country happy by his means, though he never thought that
all his labours would come to this. § 95. But he does not
speak with tears as I do. He does not believe you can be
ungrateful; he only thinks you timid. He remembers all the
honours you have done him and knows that, while the brave
man should ask for no reward, (§ 97) he has the best of all
rewards, glory. § 98. His fame has already spread to the
boundaries of the Empire. § 99. But your courage, Milo,
only makes the parting more bitter to me, and that parting
will be caused by those who should have been your best
friends.

Would I could bear your punishment! § 100. Indeed my
only consolation is that I have always been loyal to you.
§ 101. I implore the jury, I implore the soldiers not to allow a
hero like this to be expatriated. § 102. Milo, you restored

me to my country.   Must I tell my children and my brother
that I could not save you?   § 103.   Judges, do not make my
restoration more bitter to me than my banishment.   Indeed
to save Milo I could wish that Clodius were still alive.   § 104.
Heaven forbid, says he.   Will you expel this patriot, whom
every other city will delight to welcome?   § 105.   But I must
close.   Tears, which Milo will not allow, check my voice.
Judges, give your true verdict.   No one will approve such a
verdict, more than he who selected this most honourable jury.

INDEX TO NOTES.

The references are to the sections of the text.

INDEX OF NAMES.

[1] No. 4 in Smith's Class. Dict.
[2] His mother was sister to Drusus, v. § 16.

[3] Papirius was killed in attempting to recover from Clodius' followers an Armenian prince, a captive of Pompey's, whom Clodius had managed to get into his own hands.   (Asc. on § 37.)

APPENDIX

THE COMMENTARY OF ASCONIUS

ARGUMENTUM

hanc orationem dixit Cn. Pompeio III consule a. d. VI Id. April. quod iudicium cum **26** ageretur, exercitum in foro et in omnibus templis, quae circum forum sunt, collocatum a Cn. Pompeio fuisse non tantum ex oratione et annalibus, sed etiam ex libro apparet, qui Ciceronis nomine inscribitur de optimo genere oratorum. argumentum hoc est.

T. Annius Milo et P. Plautius Hypsaeus et Q. Metellus Scipio consulatum petierunt non solum largitione palam profusa, sed etiam factionibus armatorum succincti. Miloni et Clodio summae erant inimicitiae, quod et Milo Ciceronis erat amicissimus in reducendoque eo enixe operam tribunus plebis dederat, et P. Clodius restituto quoque Ciceroni erat infestissimus ideoque summe studebat Hypsaeo et Scipioni contra Milonem. ac saepe inter se Milo et Clodius cum suis factionibus Romae depugnaverant et erant uterque audacia pares, sed Milo pro melioribus partibus stabat. praeterea in eundem annum consulatum Milo, Clodius praeturam petebat, quam debilem futuram consule Milone intellegebat. inde cum diu tracta essent comitia consularia perficique ob eas ipsas perditas candidatorum **27** contentiones non possent, et ob id mense Ianuario nulli dum neque consules neque praetores essent, trahereturque dies eodem quo antea modo – cum Milo quam primum comitia confici vellet confideretque cum bonorum studiis, quod obsistebat Clodio, tum etiam populo propter effusas largitiones impensasque ludorum scaenicorum ac gladiatorii muneris maximas, in quas tria patrimonia effudisse eum Cicero significat, competitores cius trahere vellent, ideoque Pompeius, gener Scipionis, et T. Munatius tribunus plebis referri ad senatum de patriciis convocandis, qui interregem proderent, non essent passi, cum interregem prodere stata res esset –: a. d. XIII Kal. Febr. – acta etenim magis sequenda et ipsam orationem, quae actis congruit, puto quam Fenestellam, qui a. d. XIV Kal. Febr. tradit – Milo Lanuvium, ex quo erat municipio et ubi tum dictator, profectus est ad flaminem prodendum postera die. occurrit ei circa horam nonam Clodius paulo ultra Bovillas, rediens ab Aricia, prope eum locum, in quo Bonae Deae sacellum est; erat autem allocutus decuriones Aricinorum. vehebatur Clodius equo; servi XXX fere expediti, ut illo tempore mos erat iter facientibus, gladiis cincti sequebantur. erant cum Clodio praeterea tres comites eius, ex quibus eques Romanus unus, C. Causinius Schola, duo de plebe noti homines, P. Pomponius et C. Clodius. Milo raeda vehebatur cum uxore Fausta, filia L. Sullae dictatoris, et M. Saufeio, familiare suo. sequebatur eos magnum servorum agmen, **28** inter quos gladiatores quoque erant, ex quibus duo noti, Eudamus et Birria. ei in ultimo agmine tardius euntes cum servis P. Clodi rixam commiserunt. ad quem tumultum cum respexisset Clodius minitabundus, umerum eius Birria rumpia traiecit. inde cum orta esset pugna, plures Miloniani accurrerunt. Clodius vulneratus in tabernam proximam in Bovillano delatus est. Milo ut cognovit vulneratum Clodium, cum sibi periculosius illud etiam vivo eo futurum intellegeret, occiso autem magnum solacium esset habiturus etiamsi subeunda esset poena, exturbari taberna iussit. fuit antesignanus servorum eius M. Saufeius. atque ita Clodius latens extractus est multisque vulneribus confectus. cadaver eius in via relictum, quia servi Clodi aut occisi erant aut graviter saucii, aut latebant, Sex. Tedius senator, qui forte ex rure in urbem revertebatur, sustulit et lectica sua Romam ferri iussit; ipse rursus eodem, unde erat egressus, se recepit. perlatum est corpus Clodi ante primam noctis horam, infimaeque plebis et servorum maxima multitudo magno luctu corpus in atrio domus positum circumstetit. augebat autem facti invidiam uxor Clodi Fulvia, quae cum effusa lamentatione vulnera eius ostendebat. maior postera die luce prima multitudo eiusdem generis confluxit compluresque noti homines elisi sunt, inter quos C. Vibienus senator. erat domus Clodi, ante paucos menses empta de M. Scauro, in Palatio. eodem T. Munatius Plancus, frater L. Planci oratis, et Q. Pompeius Rufus, Sullae dictatoris ex filia nepos, tribuni plebis accurrerunt, eisque hortantibus vulgus imperitum corpus nudum ac lutatum, sicut in lecto erat positum, ut vulnera videri possent, in forum detulit et

29 in rostris posuit. ibi pro contione Plancus et Pompeius, qui competitoribus Milonis studebant, invidiam Miloni fecerunt. tum populus duce Sex. Clodio scriba corpus P. Clodi in curiam intulit cremavitque subselliis et tribunalibus et mensis et codicibus librariorum, quo igne et ipsa quoque curia flagravit, et item Porcia basilica, quae erat ei iuncta, ambusta est. domus quoque M. Lepidi interregis – is enim magistratus curulis erat creatus – et absentis Milonis eadem illa Clodiana multitudo oppugnavit, sed inde sagittis repulsa est. tum fasces ex luco Libitinae raptos attulit ad domum Scipionis et Hypsaei, deinde ad hortos Cn. Pompei, clamitans eum modo consulem, modo dictatorem.

incendium curiae maiorem aliquanto indignationem civitatis moverat quam interfectio Clodi. itaque Milo, quem opinio fuerat ivisse in voluntarium exsilium, invidia adversariorum recreatus nocte ea redierat Romam, qua incensa erat curia. petebatque nihil deterritus consulatum; aperte quoque tributim singula milia assium dederat. contionem ei post aliquos dies dedit M. Caelius tribunus plebis atque ipse etiam causam eius egit ad populum. dicebant uterque Miloni a Clodio factas esse insidias.

fiebant interea alii ex aliis interreges, quia comitia consularia propter eosdem candidatorum tumultus et easdem manus armatas haberi non poterant. itaque primo factum erat senatus consultum, ut interrex et tribuni plebis et Cn. Pompeius, qui pro consule ad urbem erat, viderent, ne quid detrimenti res publica caperet, dilectus autem Pompeius tota Italia haberet. qui cum summa celeritate praesidium comparasset, postulaverunt apud eum familiam Milonis, item Faustae uxoris eius exhibendam duo

30 adulescentuli, qui Appii Claudii ambo apellabantur, qui erant C. Claudi fillii, qui frater fuerat Clodi, et ob id patrui sui mortem velut auctore patre persequebantur. easdem Faustae et Milonis familias postulaverunt duo Valerii, Nepos et Leo, et L. Herennius Balbus. P. Clodio quoque familiam et comitum eius postulavit eodem tempore Caelius; familiam Hypsaei et Q. Pompei postulavit .... adfuerunt Miloni Q. Hortensius, M. Cicero, M. Marcellus, M. Calidius, M. Cato, Faustus Sulla. verba pauca Q. Hortensius fecit dixitque liberos esse eos, qui pro servis postularentur; nam post recentem caedem manu miserat eos Milo sub hoc titulo, quod caput suum ulti essent. haec agebantur mense intercalari. post diem tricesimum fere quam erat Clodius occisus Q. Metellus Scipio in senatu contra M. Caelium conquestus est de hac caede P. Clodi; falsum esse dixit, quod Milo sic se defenderet, ut insidias sibi factas esse diceret. Clodium Aricinos decuriones alloquendi gratia abisse, profectum cum sex ac viginti servis: Milonem subito post horam quartam senatu misso cum servis amplius trecentis armatis obviam ei contendisse et supra Bovillas inopinantem in itinere aggressum; ibi P. Clodium tribus vulneribus acceptis Bovillas perlatum; tabernam, in quam perfugerat, expugnatam a Milone; semianimem Clodium extractum ex taberna et in via Appia occisum esse anulumque ei morienti detractum; deinde Milonem, cum sciret in Albano parvulum filium Clodi, venisse ad villam, et cum puer ante subtractus esset, ex servo Halicore quaestionem ita habuisse, ut eum articulatim consecarent; vilicum et duos praeterea servos iugulasse; ex servis Clodi, qui

31 dominum defenderint, undecim esse interfectos; Milonis duos solos saucios factos esse; ob quae Milonem postero die duodecim servos, qui maxime operam navassent, manu misisse, populoque tributim singula milia aeris ad defendendos de se rumores dedisse. Milo mississe ad Cn. Pompeium dicebatur, qui Hypsaeo summe studebat, quod fuerat eius quaestor, desistere se petitione consulatus, si ita ei videretur; Pompeium respondisse, nemini se neque petendi neque desistendi auctorem esse, neque populi Romani potestatem aut consilio aut sententia interpellaturum. deinde per C. Lucilium qui propter M. Ciceronis familiaritatem amicus erat Miloni, egisse quoque dicebatur, ne se de hac re consulendo invidia oneraret.

inter haec cum crebresceret rumor Cn. Pompeium creari dictatorem opportere neque aliter mala civitatis sedari posse, visum est optimatibus tutius esse eum consulem sine collega creari, et cum tractata ea res esset in senatu, facto in M. Bibuli sententiam senatus consulto Pompeius ab interrege Servio Sulpicio v. Kal. Mart. mense intercalario consul creatus est statimque consulatum iniit. deinde post diem tertium de legibus novis ferendis rettulit: duas ex senatus consulto promulgavit, alteram de vi, qua nominatim caedem in Appi via factam et incendium curiae et domum M. Lepidi interregis oppugnatam comprehendit, alteram de ambitu, poena graviore et forma iudiciorum breviore; utraque enim lex prius testes dari, deinde uno die atque eodem et ab accusatore et a reo preorari iubebat, ita ut duae horae accusatori, tres reo darentur. his legibus obsistere M. Caelius tribunus plebis studiosissimus Milonis conatus est, quod et privilegium diceret in Milonem ferri et iudicia praecipitari; sed cum pertinacius legem Caelius vituperaret, eo processit irae Pompeius, ut diceret, si coactus esset, se armis rem publicam defensurum. timebat autem **32** Pompeius Milonem seu timere se simulabat: plerumque non domi suae, sed in hortis manebat, idque ipsum in superioribus, circa quos etiam magna manus militum excubabat. senatum quoque semel repente dimiserat Pompeius, quod diceret timere se adventum Milonis. dein proximo senatu P. Cornificius ferrum Milonem intra tunicam habere ad femur alligatum dixerat; postulaverat ut femur nudaret, et ille sine mora tunicam levarat. tum M. Cicero exlamaverat, omnia illi similia crimina esse quae in Milonem dicerentur alia.

deinde T. Munatius Plancus tribunus plebis produxerat in contionem M. Aemilium Philemonem, norum hominem, libertum M. Lepidi. is se dicebat pariterque secum quattuor liberos homines iter facientes supervenisse, cum Clodius occideretur, et ob id cum proclamassent, abreptos et per duos menses in villa Milonis praeclusos fuisse; eaque res, seu vera seu falsa, magnam invidiam Miloni contraxerat. itemque Munatius et Pompeius tribuni plebis in rostra produxerant triumvirum capitalem eumque interrogaverant, an Galatam, Milonis servum, caedes facientem deprehendisset. ille dormientem in taberna pro fugitivo prehensum et ad se perductum esse responderat; denuntiaverant tamen tribuni triumviro, ne servum remitteret. sed postera die Caelius tribunus plebis et Q. Manilius Cumanus collega eius ereptum e domo triumviri servum Miloni reddiderant. haec, etsi nullam de his criminibus mentionem fecit Cicero, tamen, quia ita compereram, putavi exponenda.

inter primos et Q. Pompeius et C. Sallustius et T. Munatius Plancus tribuni plebis **33** inimicissimas contiones de Milone habebant, invidiosas etiam de Cicerone, quod Milonem tanto studio defenderet; eratque maxima pars multitudinis infensa non solum Miloni, sed etiam propter invisum patrocinium Ciceroni. postea Pompeius et Sallustius in suspicione fuerunt redisse in gratiam cum Milone ac Cicerone. Plancus autem infestissime perstitit atque in Ciceronem quoque multitudinem instigavit, Cn. Pompeio autem suspectum faciebat Milonem, ad perniciem eius comparari vim vociferatus; Pompeiusque ob ea saepius querebatur, sibi quoque fieri insidias, et id palam, ac maiore manu se armabat. dicturum quoque diem Ciceroni Plancus ostendebat, posteaquam Q. Pompeius idem meditatus erat. tanta tamen constantia ac fides fuit Ciceronis, ut non populi a se alienatione, non Cn. Pompei suspicionibus, non periculo futurum ut sibi dies ad populum diceretur, non armis, quae palam in Milonem sumpta erant, deterreri potuerit a defensione eius, cum posset omne periculum suum et offensionem inimicae sibi multitudinis declinare, redimere autem Cn. Pompei animum, si paulum ex studio defensionis remisisset.

perlata deinde lege Pompeia, in qua id quoque scriptum erat, ut quaesitor suffragio populi ex iis, qui consules fuerant, crearetur, statim comitia habita creatusque est L. Domitius Ahenobarbus quaesitor. Album quoque iudicum, qui de ea re iudicarent, **34** Pompeius tale proposuit, ut numquam neque clariores viros neque sanctiores propositos esse constaret. post quod statim nova lege Milo postulatus a duobus Appiis Claudiis adulescentibus, isdem a quibus antea familia eius fuerat postulata, itemque de ambitu ab isdem Appiis et praeterea a . . . , de vi a Q. Patulcio et L. Cornificio, de sodaliciis a P. Fulvio Nerato. postulatus autem erat et de sodaliciis et de ambitu ea spe, quod primum iudicium de vi futurum apparebat, quo eum damnatum iri confidebant nec postea responsurum.

divinatio de ambitu accusatorum facta est quaesitore A. Torquato, atque ambo quaesitores, Torquatus et Domitius, pridie Non. April. reum adesse iusserunt. quo die Milo ad Domiti tribunal venit, ad Torquati amicos misit; ibi postulante pro eo M. Marcello obtinuit, ne prius causam de ambitu diceret, quam de vi iudicium esset perfectum. apud Domitium autem quaesitorem maior Appius postulavit a Milone servos exhiberi numero III et L, et cum ille negaret eos qui nominabantur in sua potestate esse, Domitius ex sententia iudicum pronuntiavit, ut ex servorum suorum numero accusator quot vellet ederet. citati deinde testes secundum legem, quae, ut supra diximus, iubebat, ut prius quam causa ageretur, testes per triduum audirentur, dicta eorum iudices confirmarent, quarta die adesse omnes iuberentur, ac coram accusatore ac reo pilae, in quibus nomina iudicum inscripta essent, aequarentur; dein rursus sortitio iudicum fieret, unius et LXXX: qui numerus cum sorte obtigisset, ipsi protinus sessum irent; tum ad dicendum accusator duas horas, reus tres haberet, resque eodem die illo iudicaretur; prius autem quam sententiae ferrentur, quinos **35** ex singulis ordinibus accusator, totidem reus reiceret, ita ut numerus iudicum relinqueretur, qui sententias ferrent, quinquaginta et unus.

primo die datus erat in Milonem testis Causinius Schola, qui se cum P. Clodio fuisse, cum is occisus esset, dixit, atrocitatemque rei factae quam maxime potuit auxit. quem cum interrogare M. Marcellus coepisset, tanto tumultu Clodianae multitudinis circumstantis exterritus est, ut vim ultimam timens in tribunal a Domitio reciperetur. quam ob causam Marcellus et ipse Milo a Domitio praesidium imploraverunt. sedebat eo tempore Cn. Pompeius ad aerarium perturbatusque erat eodem illo clamore; itaque Domitio promisit se postero die cum praesidio descensurum, idque fecit. qua re territi Clodiani silentio verba testium per biduum audiri passi sunt. interrogaverunt eos M. Cicero et M. Marcellus et Milo ipse. multi ex eis, qui Bovillis habitabant, testimonium dixerunt de eis, quae ibi facta erant: cauponem occisum, tabernam expugnatam, corpus Clodi in publicum extractum esse. virgines quoque Albanae dixerunt mulierem ignotam venisse ad se, quae Milonis mandato votum solveret, quod Clodius occisus esset. ultimae testimonium dixerunt Sempronia, Tuditani filia, socrus P. Clodi, et uxor Fulvia, et fletu suo magnopere eos qui adsistebant commoverunt. dimisso circa horam decimam iudicio T. Munatius pro contione populum adhortatus est, ut postero die frequens adesset et elabi Milonem non pateretur iudiciumque et dolorem suum ostenderet euntibus ad tabellam ferendam. postero die, qui fuit iudicii **36** summus a. d. VII Id. April., clausae fuerunt tota urbe tabernae; praesidia in foro et circa omnes fori aditus Pompeius disposuit; ipse pro aerario, ut pridie, consedit saeptus delecta manu militum. sortitio deinde iudicum a primo die facta est; post tantum silentium toto foro fuit, quantum esse in aliquo foro potest. tum intra horam secundam accusatores coeperunt dicere, Appius maior et M. Antonius et P. Valerius Nepos; usi sunt ex lege horis duabus.

respondit his unus M. Cicero; et cum quibusdam placuisset ita defendi crimen, interfici Clodium pro re publica fuisse (quam formam M. Brutus secutus est in ea oratione, quam pro Milone composuit et edidit, quasi egisset), Ciceroni id non placuit, quasi qui bono publico damnari, idem etiam occidi indemnatus posset. itaque cum insidias Milonem Clodio fecisse posuissent accusatores, quia falsum id erat (nam forte illa rixa commissa fuerat), Cicero apprehendit et contra Clodium Miloni fecisse insidias disputavit, eoque tota oratio eius spectavit. sed ita constitit, ut diximus, neutrius consilio pugnatum esse eo die, verum et forte occurrisse et ex rixa servorum ad caedem perventum. notum tamen erat utrumque mortem alteri saepe minatum esse, et sicut suspectum Milonem maior quam Clodi familia faciebat, ita expeditior et paratior ad pugnam Clodianorum quam Milonis fuerat. Cicero cum inciperet dicere, exceptus acclamatione Clodianorum, qui se continere ne metu quidem circumstantium militum potuerunt; itaque non ea qua solitus erat constantia dixit. manet autem illa quoque excepta eius oratio. scripsit vero hanc quam legimus, ita pefecte, ut iure prima haberi possit.

ENARRATIO

(§ 3.) *'unum genus est adversum infestumque nobis'* et cetera.   **37**

ita ut in causae expositione diximus, Munatius Plancus pridie pro contione populum adhortatus erat, ne pateretur elabi Milonem.

(§ 12.) *'declarant huius ambusti tribuni plebis illae inter mortuae contiones, quibus quotidie meam potentiam invidiose criminabatur.'*

T. Munatius Plancus et Q. Pompeius Rufus tribuni plebis, de quibus in argumento huius orationis diximus, cum contra Milonem Scipioni et Hypsaeo studerent, contionati sunt eo ipso tempore plebemque in Milonem accenderunt, quo propter Clodi corpus curia incensa est, nec prius destiterunt, quam flamma eius incendii fugati sunt e contione. erant enim tunc rostra non eo loco quo nunc sunt, sed ad comitium, prope iuncta curiae. ob hoc T. Munatium ambustum tribunum appellat; fuit autem paratus ad dicendum.

(§ 13.) *'cur igitur incendium curiae, oppugnationem aedium M. Lepidi, caedem hanc ipsam contra rem publicam senatus factam esse decrevit?'*

post biduum medium quam Clodius occisus erat, interrex primus proditus est M. Aemilius Lepidus. non fuit autem moris ab eo, qui primus interrex proditus erat, comitia haberi. sed Scipionis et Hypsaei factiones, quia recens invidia Milonis erat, cum contra ius postularent, ut interrex ad comitia consulum creandorum descenderet, idque ipse non **38** faceret, domum eius per omnes interregni dies (fuerunt autem ex more quinque) obsederunt. deinde omni vi ianua expugnata et imagines maiorum deiecerunt et lectulum adversum uxoris eius Corneliae, cuius castitas pro exemplo habita est, fregerunt, itemque telas, quae ex vetere more in atrio texebantur, diruerunt. post quae supervenit Milonis manus et ipsa postulans comitia; cuius adventus fuit saluti Lepido: in se enim ipsae conversae sunt factiones inimicae, atque ita oppugnatio domus interregis omissa est.

(§ 14.) *'quod si per furiosum illum tribunum plebis senatui quod sentiebat perficere licuisset, novam quaestionem nullam haberemus. decernebat enim, ut veteribus legibus, tantummodo extra ordinem, quaereretur. divisa sententia est postulante nescio quo. sic reliqua auctoritas senatus empta intercessione sublata est.'*

quid sit 'dividere sententiam', ut enarrandum sit, vestra aetas, filii, facit.

cum aliquis in dicenda sententia duas pluresve res complectitur, si cui non omnes eae probantur, postulat ut dividatur, id est de rebus singulis referatur. forsitan nunc hoc quoque velitis scire, qui fuerit, qui id postulaverit. quod non fere traditur: non enim ei, qui hoc postulat, oratione longa utendum ac ne consurgendum quidem utique est; multi enim **39** sedentes hoc unum verbum pronuntiant 'divide': quod cum auditum est, liberum est ei, qui facit relationem, dividere. sed ego, ut curiosius aetati vestrae satisfaciam, acta etiam totius illius temporis persecutus sum; in quibus cognovi pridie Kal. Mart. senatus consultum esse factum, P. Clodi caedem et incendium curiae et oppugnationem aedium M. Lepidi contra rem publicam factam; ultra relatum in actis illo die nihil; postero die, id est Kal. Mart., T. Munatium in contione exposuisse populo quae pridie acta erant in senatu: in qua contione haec dixit ad verbum: 'cum Hortensius dixisset, ut extra ordinem quaereretur apud quaesitorem; aestimare futurum, ut, cum pusillum edissent dulcedinis, largiter acerbitatis devorarent: adversus hominem ingeniosum non ingenio usi sumus; invenimus Fufium, qui diceret "divide"; reliquae parti sententiae ego et Sallustius intercessimus'. haec contio, ut puto, explicat, et quid senatus decernere voluerit, et quis divisionem postulaverit, et quis intercesserit et cur. illud vos meminisse non dubito per Q. Fufium illo quoque tempore quo de incesto P. Clodi actum est factum, ne a senatu asperius decerneretur.

de L. Domitio dicit;

(§ 22.) *'dederas enim, quam contemneres populares insanias, iam ab adulescentia documenta maxima.'*

40   constantiam L. Domiti quam in praetura praestitit significat. nam eo tempore, cum C. Manilius tribunus plebis subnixus libertinorum et servorum manu perditissimam legem ferret, ut libertinis in omnibus tribubus suffragium esset, idque per tumultum ageret et clivum Capitolinum obsideret, discusserat perruperatque coetum Domitius ita, ut multi Manilianorum interficerentur. quo facto et plebem infimam offenderat et senatus magnam gratiam inierat.

(§ 32). *'itaque illud Cassianum iudicium in his personis valeat.'*

L. Cassius fuit, sicut iam saepe diximus, summae vir severitatis. is quotiens quaesitor iudicii alicuius esset, in quo quaerebatur de homine occiso, suadebat atque etiam praeibat iudicibus hoc, quod Cicero nunc admonet, ut quaereretur, cui bono fuisset perire eum de cuius morte quaeritur. ob quam severitatem, quo tempore Sex. Peducaeus tribunus plebis criminatus est L. Metellum pontificem maximum totumque collegium pontificum male iudicasse de incesto virginum Vestalium, quod unam modo Aemiliam damnaverat, absolverat autem duas Marciam et Liciniam, populus hunc Cassium creavit qui de eisdem virginibus quaereret: isque et utrasque eas et praeterea complures alias nimia etiam, ut existimatio est, asperitate usus damnavit.

(§ 33.) *'et aspexit me illis quidem oculis, quibus tunc solebat, cum omnibus omnia minabatur. movet me quippe lumen curiae!'*

hic est Sex. Clodius, quem in argumento huius orationis diximus corpus Clodi in curiam attulisse et ibi cremasse eoque incenso curiam conflagrasse; ideo lumen curiae dicit.

(§ 37.) *'quando illius postea sica illa, quam a Catilina acceperat, conquievit? haec intentata nobis est, huic ego obici vos pro me non sum passus, haec insidiata Pompeio est.'*

41   quod dicit 'intentata nobis est et obici vos pro me non sum passus', manifestum est pertinere ad id tempus, quo post rogationem a P. Clodio in eum promulgatam urbe cessit. quare dicat 'insidiata Pompeio est', fortassis quaeritis. Pisone et Gabinio consulibus, pulso Cicerone in exilium, cum III Id. Sex. Pompeius in senatum venit, dicitur servo P. Clodi sica excidisse, eaque ad Gabinium consulem delata dictum est servo imperatum a P. Clodio, ut Pompeius occideretur. Pompeius statim domum rediit et ex eo domi se tenuit. obsessus est etiam a liberto Clodi Damione, ut ex actis eius anni cognovi, in quibus XV Kal. Sept. L. Novius tribunus plebis, collega Clodi, cum Damio adversum L. Flavium praetorem appellaret tribunos et tribuni de appellatione cognoscerent, ita sententiam dixit: 'etsi ab hoc apparitore P. Clodi vulneratus sum, et hominibus armatis praesidiis dispositis a republica remotus Cn. Pompeius obsessusque est: cum appeller, non utar eius exemplo, quem vitupero, et iudicium tollam', et reliqua de intercessione.

'haec viam Appiam monumentum nominis sui nece Papiri cruentavit.'

Pompeius post triumphum Mithridaticum Tigranis filium in catenis deposuerat apud
Flavium senatorem: qui postea cum esset praetor eodem anno, quo tribunus plebis **42**
Clodius, petiit ab eo Clodius super cenam, ut Tigranem adduci iuberet, ut eum videret.
adductum collocavit in convivio, dein Flavio non reddidit Tigranem; domi suae habuit
extra catenas nec repetenti Pompeio reddidit. postea in navem deposuit, et cum
profugeret ille, tempestate delatus est Antium. inde ut deduceretur ad se, Clodius Sex.
Clodium, de quo supra diximus, misit. qui cum reduceret, Flavius quoque re cognita ad
deripiendum Tigranem profectus est. ad quartum lapidem ab urbe pugna facta est, in
qua multi ex utraque parte ceciderunt, plures tamen ex Flavi, inter quos et M. Papirius
eques Romanus, publicanus, familiaris Pompeio. Flavius sine comite Romam vix
perfugit.

*'Haec eadem longo intervallo conversa rursus est in me: nuper quidem, ut scitis, me
ad regiam paene confecit.'*

quo die periculum hoc dierit, ut Clodius eum ad regiam paene confecerit, nusquam
inveni; non tamen adducor ut putem Ciceronem mentitum, praesertim cum adiciat ut
scitis. sed videtur mihi loqui de eo die, quo consulibus Domitio et Messalla, qui
praecesserant eum annum, cum haec oratio dicta est, inter candidatorum Hypsaei et
Milonis manus in via Sacra pugnatum est, multique ex Milonis ex improviso ceciderunt.
de cuius diei periculo suo ut putem loqui eum, facit et locus pugnae (nam in Sacra via
traditur commissa, in qua est regia), et quod adsidue simul erant cum candidatis
suffragatores, Milonis Cicero, Hypsaei Clodius.

(§ 38.) *'potuitne L. Caecili, iustissimi fortissimique praetoris, obpugnata domo?'* **43**

L. Caecilius Rufus, de quo dicitur, fuit praetor P. Lentulo Spinthere Q. Metello Nepote
consulibus, quo anno Cicero restitutus est. is cum faceret ludos Apollinares, ita infima
coacta multitudo annonae caritate tumultuata est, ut omnes, qui in theatro spectandi
causa consederant, pellerentur. de oppugnata domo nusquam adhuc legi; Pompeius
tamen cum defenderet Milonem apud populum, de vi accusante Clodio, obiecit, ut
legimus apud Tironem libertum Ciceronis in libro IV de vita eius, oppressum a Clodio L.
Caecilium praetorem.

(§ 45.) *'at quo die? quo, ut ante dixi, fuit insanissima contio, ab ipsius mercennario
tribuno plebis concitata.'*

hoc significat eo die quo Clodius occisus est contionatum esse mercennarium eius
tribunum plebis. sunt autem contionati eo die, ut ex actis apparet, C. Sallustius et Q.
Pompeius, utrique et inimici Milionis et satis inquieti. sed videtur mihi Q. Pompeium
significare; nam eius seditiosior fuit contio.

(§ 46.) *'dixit C. Causinius Schola Interamnanus, familiarissimus et idem comes Clodi,
P. Clodium illo die in Albano mansurum fuisse.'*

hic fuit Causinius, apud quem Clodius mansisse Interamnae videri volebat qua nocte
deprehensus est in Caesaris domo, cum ibi in operto virgines pro populo Romano sacra
facerent.

(§ 47.) *'scitis, iudices, fuisse, qui in hac rogatione suadenda diceret Milonis manu* **44**
*caedem esse factam, consilio vero maioris alicuius. me videlicet latronem et sicarium
abiecti homines et perditi describebant.'*

Q. Pompeius Rufus et C. Sallustius tribuni fuerunt quos significat. hi enim primi de ea
lege ferenda populum hortati sunt et dixerunt a manu Milonis occisum esse Clodium,
consilio vero maioris alicuius.

(§ 49.) *'atqui ut illi nocturnus adventus vitandus fuit, sic Miloni, cum insidiator esset,
si illum ad urbem noctu accessurum sciebat, subsidendum'* et cetera.

Via Appia est prope urbem monumentum Basili, qui locus latrociniis fuit perinfamis,
quod ex aliis quoque multis intellegi potest.

(§ 55.) *'comites Graeculi quocumque ibat, etiam cum in castra Etrusca properabat.'*

saepe obiecit Clodio Cicero socium eum coniurationis Catilinae fuisse; quam rem nunc quoque reticens ostendit. fuerat enim opinio, ut Catilina ex urbe profugerat in castra Manli centurionis, qui tum in Etruria ad Faesulas exercitum ei comparabat, Clodium subsequi eum voluisse et coepisse, tum dein mutato consilio in urbem redisse.

(§ 67.) *'non iam hoc Clodianum crimen timemus, sed tuas, Cn. Pompei, te enim appello, et ea voce, ut me exaudire possis, tuas, inquam, suspiciones perhorrescimus.'*

45 diximus in argumento orationis huius Cn. Pompeium simulasse timorem, seu plane timuisse Milonem, et ideo ne domi quidem suae, sed in hortis superioribus ante iudicium mansisse, ita ut villam quoque praesidio militum circumdaret. Q. Pompeius Rufus tri-bunus plebis, qui fuerat familiarissimus omnium P. Clodio et sectam eam sequi se palam profitebatur, dixerat in contione paucis post diebus quam Clodius erat occisus: 'Milo dedit quem in curia cremaretis: dabit, quem in Capitolio sepeliatis'. in eadem contione idem dixerat – habuit enim eam a. d. VIII Kal. Febr. – cum Milo pridie, id est IX Kal. Febr., venire ad Pompeium in hortis eius voluisset, Pompeium ei per hominem propinquum misisse nuntium, ne ad se veniret. prius etiam quam Pompeius III consul crearetur, tres tribuni, Q. Pompeius Rufus, C. Sallustius Crispus, T. Munatius Plancus, cum quotidianis contionibus suis magnam invidiam Miloni propter occisum Clodium excitarent, produxerant ad populum Cn. Pompeium et ab eo quaesierant, num ad eum delatum esset illius quoque rei indicium, suae vitae insidiari Milonem. responderat Pompeius: Licinium quendam de plebe sacrificulum, qui solitus esset familias purgare, ad se detulisse servos quosdam Milonis itemque libertos comparatos esse ad caedem suam, nomina quoque servorum edidisse; se ad Milonem misisse, ut eos in potestae sua haberet; a Milone responsum esse, ex eis servis quos nominasset partim neminem se unquam habuisse, partim manumisisse; dein, cum Licinium apud se haberet, ...Lucium quendam de plebe ad corrumpendum indicem venisse; qua re cognita in

46 vincla eum publica esse coniectum. decreverat enim senatus ut cum interrege et tribunis plebis Pompeius daret operam, ne quid res publica detrimenti caperet. ob has suspiciones Pompeius in superioribus hortis se continuerat; deinede ex senatus consulto dilectu per Italiam habito cum redisset, venientem ad se Milonem unum omnium non admiserat. item cum senatus in porticu Pompeii haberetur, ut Pompeius posset interesse, unum eum excuti prius quam in senatum intraret iusserat. hae sunt suspiciones quas se Cicero dicit pertimescere.

(§ 71.) *'quid enim minus illo dignum quam cogere, ut vos eum condemnetis, in quem animadvertere ipse et more maiorum et suo iure posset? sed praesidio esse' et cetera.*

idem T. Munatius Plancus, ut saepe diximus, post audita et obsignata testium verba dimissosque interim iudices vocata contione cohortatus erat populum, ut clusis tabernis postero die ad iudicium adesset nec pateretur elabi Milonem.

(§ 87.) *'incidebantur iam domi leges, quae nos servis nostris addicerent.'*

significasse iam puto nos fuisse inter leges P. Clodi, quas ferre proposuerat, eam quoque, que libertini, qui non plus quam in IV tribubus sufragium ferebant, possent in rusticis quoque tribunus, quae propriae ingenuorum sunt, ferre.

(§ 88.) *'senatus, credo, praetorem eum circumscrisisset. ne cum solebat quidem id facere, in privato eodem hoc aliquid profecerat.'*

47 significat id tempus quo P. Clodius, cum adhuc quaestor designatus esset, deprensus est, cum intrasset eo, ubi sacrificium pro populo Romano fiebat. quod factum notatum erat gravi senatus consulto, decretumque extra ordinem de ea re iudicium fieret ...

quo loco inducit loquentem Milonem cum bonarum partium hominibus de meritis suis;

(§ 95.) *'plebem et infimam multitudinem, quae P. Clodio duce fortunis vestris imminebat, eam, quo tutior esset vestra vita, se fecisse commemorat ut non modo virtute flecteret, sed etiam tribus suis patrimoniis deleniret.'*

puto iam supra esse dictum Milonem ex familia fuisse Papia, deinde adtoptatum esse ab T. Annio, avo suo materno. tertium patrimonium videtur significare matris; aliud enim quod fuerit, non invenio.

peracta utrimque causa singuli quinos accusator et reus senatores, totidem equites et tribunos aerarios reiecerunt, ita ut unus et L sententias tulerint. senatores condemnaverunt XII, absolverunt VI; equites condemnaverunt XIII, absolverunt IV; tribuni aerarii condemnaverunt XIII, absolverunt III. videbantur non ignorasse iudices inscio Milone initio vulneratum esse Clodium, sed compererant post quam vulneratus esset iussu Milonis occisum. fuerunt qui crederent M. Catonis sententia eum esse absolutum; nam et bene cum re publica actum esse morte P. Clodi non dissimulaverat et studebat in petitione consulatus Miloni et reo adfuerat. nominaverat quoque eum Cicero praesentem et testatus erat audisse eum a M. Favonio ante diem tertium quam facta caedes erat, Clodium dixisse periturum esse eo triduo Milonem . . . sed Milonis quoque **48** notam audaciam removeri a re publica utile visum est. scire tamen nemo umquam potuit, utram sententiam tulisset. damnatum autem opera maxime Appi Claudi pronuntiatum est. Milo postero die nova lege factus reus ambitus apud Manlium Torquatum absens damnatus est. illa quoque lege accusator fuit eius Appius Claudius, et cum ei praemium lege daretur, negavit se eo uti. subscripserunt ei in ambitus iudicio P. Valerius Leo et Cn. Domitius Cn. filius. post paucos dies quoque Milo apud M. Favonium quaesitorem de sodaliciis damnatus est accusante P. Fulvio Nerato, cui e lege praemium datum est. deinde apud L. Fabium quaesitorem iterum absens damnatus est de vi: accusavit L. Cornificius et Q. Patulcius. Milo in exilium Massiliam intra paucissimos dies profectus est. bona eius propter aeris alieni magnitudinem semuncia venierunt.

post Milonem eadem lege Pompeia primus est accusatus M. Saufeius M. filius, qui dux fuerat in expugnanda taberna Bovillis et Clodio occidendo. accusaverunt eum L. Cassius, L. Fulcinius C. filius, C. Valerius; defenderunt M. Cicero, M. Caelius, obtinueruntque ut una sententia absolveretur. condemnaverunt senatores X, absolverunt VIII; condemnaverunt equites Romani IX, absolverunt VIII; sed ex tribunis aerariis X absolverunt, VI damnaverunt: manifestumque odium Clodi saluti Saufeio fuit, cum eius vel peior causa quam Milonis fuisset, quod aperte dux fuerat expugnandae **49** tabernae. repetitus deinde post paucos dies apud C. Considium quaesitorem est lege Plautia de vi, subscriptione ea quod loca publica occupasset et cum telo fuisset; nam dux fuerat operarum Milonis. accusaverunt C. Fidius, Cn. Aponius Cn. filius, M. Seius . . . Sex. filius; defenderunt M. Cicero, M. Terentius Varro Gibba. absolutus est sententiis plenius quam prius: graves habuit XIX, absolutorias duas et XXX; sed e contrario hoc ac priore iudicio accidit: equites enim ac senatores eum absolverunt, tribuni aerari damnaverunt.

Sex. autem Clodius, quo auctore corpus Clodi in curiam illatum fuit, accusantibus C. Caesennio Philone, M. Alfidio, defendente T. Flacconio, magno consensu damnatus est, sententiis sex et XL; absolutorias quinque omnino habuit, duas senatorum, tres equitum.

multi praeterea et praesentes et cum citati non respondissent damnati sunt: ex quibus maxima pars fuit Clodianorum.

BRISTOL CLASSICAL PRESS

LATIN LIST

ADVANCED LATIN UNSEENS
Drawn from the selection of COOK and MARCHANT by ANTHONY BOWEN

AMMIANUS MARCELLINUS; A Selection
Text with Introduction and Notes by R. C. BLOCKLEY

CICERO: *PHILIPPICS I & II*
Edited by J. D. DENNISTON

CICERO: *PRO MILONE*
Edited with Introduction and Notes by F. H. COLSON

CICERO: *VERRINE V*
Edited with Introduction, Notes and Vocabulary by R. G. C. LEVENS

HORACE IN HIS *ODES*
Selected *Odes* with running Commentary and Vocabularies by J. A. HARRISON

JUVENAL: *SATIRES I, III, X*
Text with Introduction and Notes by N. RUDD and E. COURTNEY

LATIN LOVE ELEGY
Selections with Introduction and Notes by R. MALTBY

LUCAN: *DE BELLO CIVILI VII*
Text with Introduction and Notes by O. A. W. DILKE

OVID: *AMORES I*
Edited with Translation and running Commentary by JOHN BARSBY

OVID: *METAMORPHOSES III*
Text with Introduction, Notes and Vocabulary by A. A. R. HENDERSON

OVID: *METAMORPHOSES XI*
Edited with Introduction, Notes and Vocabulary by G. M. H. MURPHY

RES PUBLICA: Roman Politics and Society according to Cicero
By W. K. LACEY & B. W. J. G. WILSON

ROMAN DECLAMATION
Texts with Introduction and Notes by MICHAEL WINTERBOTTOM

SALLUST: *BELLUM CATILINAE*
Text with Introduction and Notes by PATRICK McGUSHIN

SALLUST: ROME AND JUGURTHA
Text with Introduction and Notes by J. R. HAWTHORN

SENECA THE YOUNGER: Selected Prose
Texts with Introduction and Notes by H. MacL. CURRIE

SILVER LATIN EPIC: An Approach
Texts with Introduction and Notes by H. MacL. CURRIE

SUETONIUS: *DIVUS AUGUSTUS*
Text with Introduction and Notes by J. M. CARTER

SUETONIUS: *NERO*
Text with Introduction and Notes by B. H. WARMINGTON .

VIRGIL: *AENEID VIII*
Edited by H. E. GOULD and J. L. WHITELEY

VIRGIL: *AENEID IX*
Edited by J. L. WHITELEY

VIRGIL: *GEORGICS I & IV*
Edited by H. H. HUXLEY

BRISTOL CLASSICAL PRESS

GREEK   LIST

ADVANCED GREEK UNSEENS
Drawn from the selection of COOK and MARCHANT and edited by ANTHONY BOWEN

EURIPIDES: *HECUBA*
Text with Introduction, Notes and Vocabulary by M. TIERNEY

EURIPIDES: SCENES FROM *TROJAN WOMEN*
Text with Introduction, Notes and Vocabulary by F. KINCHIN SMITH & B. HODGE

ESSENTIAL HESIOD
Theogony 1–232 and 453–733, *Erga* 1–302 with Introduction and Notes by C. J. ROWE

HOMER: *ILIAD III*
Text with Introduction, Notes and Vocabulary by J. T. HOOKER

HOMER: *ODYSSEY IX*
Text with Introduction and running Vocabulary by J. V. MUIR

LINEAR B: An Introduction
By J. T. HOOKER

LUCIAN: A Selection
Text with Introduction, Notes and Vocabulary by K. C. SIDWELL

LYSIAS: FIVE SPEECHES
Orations 10, 12, 14, 19 and 22 edited with Introduction and Notes by E. S. SHUCKBURGH

PLATO: THE STORY OF ATLANTIS
Timaeus 17–27 and *Critias* 106–121 with Introduction, Notes and Vocabulary by CHRISTOPHER GILL

THUCYDIDES: BOOK I Chapters 1–55
Edited by E. C. MARCHANT with new Introduction and Bibliography by THOMAS WIEDEMANN

THUCYDIDES: BOOK II
Edited by E. C. MARCHANT with new Introduction and Bibliography by THOMAS WIEDEMANN

XENOPHON: THE FALL OF ATHENS
Selections from *Hellenika* I & II with Introduction, Notes and Vocabulary by T. HORN

XENOPHON: THE PERSIAN EXPEDITION
Anabasis selections with Introduction, Notes and Vocabulary by J. ANTRICH & S. USHER